CHANA
A Life in Prayer

With abiding admiration

CHANA
A Life in Prayer

Rabbi Yehiel E. Poupko

AN ARTHUR KURZWEIL BOOK
New York/Jerusalem

AN ARTHUR KURZWEIL BOOK
11 Bond Street #456
Great Neck, NY 11021

First edition

Cover and interior design by Judith M. Tulli.

Rabbi Yehiel E. Poupko
Chana
A Life in Prayer

ISBN: 978-0-692-88898-8

A review of the prayerful life of Chana
In Sefer Shemuel
Its presentation by Hazal
And its meaning for the Yamim Nora'im

In Memoriam
Chana Tova Poupko
7 Adar 5772 9 Sivan 5774

לזכר נשמת נכדתי
חנה טובה ע"ה
בת
הרב חיים ליב דוד שלמה
ואסתר שושנה פופקא יצ"ו
ז' אדר תשע"ב ט'סיון תשע"ד
האהובה והנעימה בחייה
ובמותה לא נפרדנו ממנה
מאת סבה המאן להתנחם
יחיאל אפרים פופקא

Table of Contents

לעדה המצבה הזאת

בשבת ט' סיון תשע"ד פרשת 'בהעלותך את הנרות אל מול פני המנורה יאירו...' החזירה חנה טובה ע"ה בת הרב חיים ליב דוד שלמה ואסתר שושנה יצ'ו את נשמתה הטהורה והזכה לזוהר הרקיע ולחיק בוראה הד"ה נר ה' נשמת אדם. ונפסקה שירת חייה. כשהורים קוראים שם לבת ישראל לא רק שהם נותנים לה שם אלא באותו רגע עת נצבים מול ספר התורה ומכריזים 'ויקרא שמה בישראל...' הם מגלים שרש נשמת בתם. קריאת שם מגלה את שרש הנשמה. שרש הנשמה נעוץ באותה אשה במקרא שעל שמה נקראת הבת הנולדה, אותה האשה שהקימה לראשונה את שמה לשם ולתפארת בישראל, וטבעה בשמה את קורות חייה והליכות דרכיה עם הקב"ה ובית ישראל. ואותה תינוקת נושאת שם עתיק יומין וקולה של אותה אשה ששמה נרשמת בתוכה. ואותה תינוקת מסוגלת להמשיך אורה וקולה. בתנו התינוקת היתה לנו וראו איננה ושירת חייה נפסקה. הלא היא שירת האם הנביאה, חנה אם שמואל שעלי נבואות שירה הוקמה מלכות בית דוד ומשיח אלהי ישראל. עלינו המשפחה המתאבלת להמשיך ולשיר את שירת חנה, קולה ישמע, ולהפיץ שפע אורה הזורחת מתוך תפילות המחזור מכסה לעשור.ועלינו להעיד כשאנו עומדים נוכח המקדש ושופכים שיח לפני קוננו מדי יום ביומו שעוד נראית לפנינו דמות דיוקנה של האשה המתפללת האם חנה.

On Shabbat, the ninth of Sivan 5774 — Parashat Beha'alotekha: "When you raise up and kindle the lights, let the seven lamps give light at the front of the menora" — Chana Tova, daughter of Rabbi Chaim and Dr. Shoshana Poupko, returned her soul, pure and innocent, to the radiance of the Heavens and to the bosom of her Creator, as it is written, "The soul of a person is the light of God." And her life's song was cut off.

When parents declare a name for a daughter in Israel, it is not just that they are giving her an appellation. Rather, in that moment as they stand in the presence of the Sefer Torah and declare, "And let her name be known in Israel," they are revealing the root of their daughter's soul. The chosen name reveals the source of the soul. The root of the soul emanates from the woman in TaNaKh whose name is now placed upon the baby girl — that woman who established her name as a byword in Israel, who engraved in her name her life saga and the path she walked with God and the House of Israel. This baby girl now bears a venerable name, and with it comes the ancient voice of the one for whom she is named. This newborn is destined to continue the light and voice of her namesake.

Our daughter, Chana Tova, a baby girl we had, and mark well she is no more. The song of her life is silenced. Hers was the song of the matriarch and prophetess Chana, mother of Shemuel, through whose prophecies the monarchy of the House of David and the Messiah of the God of Israel were established. It is upon us, the mourning family, to take up the silenced voice of our daughter, to continue to sing the Song of Chana so her voice will be heard, and to spread the flow of her light that radiates from the prayers of the Makhzor of Rosh HaShana and Yom Kippur. It is for us to bear witness when we stand facing the Mishkan, pouring forth our prayer before our Creator from day to day, that there yet appears before us an image of the likeness of that prayerful woman, the matriarch Chana.

Foreword

I am not an author of books. At best I write short essays, articles, and a few poems.

Yet this appears to be a book. In truth it is merely a record of my learning in the summer of 5774. On the ninth of Sivan 5774, my granddaughter, Chana Tova, daughter of Rabbi Chaim and Dr. Shoshana Poupko, died at the age of 27 months. In the weeks following her death I did not know what to do with myself. I was in *aveilut*, mourning, but I was not, in the halakhic sense, an *aveyl*, a mourner. My grandparents, who suffered much in the Soviet Union, left me a great legacy that was taught to me by my parents: In the face of torment, seek shelter in Torah learning.

תהלים פרק קיט (צב) לוּלֵי תוֹרָתְךָ שַׁעֲשֻׁעָי אָז אָבַדְתִּי בְעָנְיִי

Had not Your Torah been my delight, I would have perished in my torment (Tehilim 119:92).

That summer, lacking rituals as vessels for *aveilut*, I began to learn about Chana in TaNaKh, in Hazal, and in the Makhzor. I pursued the remarkable and compelling person and spiritual life of Chana based on an old Jewish belief: Every Jew's soul has a root, a source. The wellspring of the soul is that person in TaNaKh who bequeaths his or her name to the sons and daughters of Israel. I was driven to learn the source of my granddaughter Chana and who she would have become had she been given the years of life promised in Tehilim 90.

Learning about the biblical Chana brought me to a realization of the remarkable woman my granddaughter would have become. In learning, I took notes and discussed ideas with a few friends, who encouraged me to compose a short monograph for Rosh HaShana and Yom Kippur 5775. I did so. The friends who read the monograph urged me to expand it into a book.

First and foremost, this book is a *tefila*, a prayer, for Chana's parents, my children Chaim and Shoshana. In the darkest of life experiences they presented wisdom, goodness, and faith that their parents never wanted to know they possessed. This book is written so that Chana's sisters, Ayelet and Elana, will for all time know the spiritual life of their baby sister, whom they called Babu. This book is written so that Chana's cousins — Shemuel Meir, Ayelet, and Atara Poupko; Amitai, Erez, and Gadi Schreiber; Sarah, Yonatan, Ariel, and Hinda Segal — will ever remember her. It is my aspiration that as my grandchildren meet Chana, year in and year out, in the pages of the Makhzor on Rosh HaShana and Yom Kippur, they will keep this book with them and remember their cousin, Chana Tova, the spark of whose soul is bequeathed by Chana, the Mother of Jewish prayer.

Acknowledgments

Many learned friends of mine read the manuscript of this book. I was helped in an early version, when it was a small monograph, by Abe Friedman, Joel Hecker, and Ben Katz.

I received important help from Saul Berman, Donniel Hartman, Helene Lerner, Leonard Matanky, Daniel Matt, Ronit Meroz, Aharon David Segal, and Avigdor Shinan. I benefited from several conversations with Shalom Holtz. Jon Levenson saved me from many an error, and helped to refine many an idea.

Without the help of my wise and learned friend Margy-Ruth Davis, who has brought so very many of the writings of HaRav Adin Steinsaltz to print, this book would not have come to be. Margy-Ruth identified a publisher who would adopt this book. Margy-Ruth read through the entire manuscript at least twice, giving me the benefit of her insight and thoughtfulness in copious notes on virtually every page. She brought about the complete reorganization of the first and second versions of the manuscript. She has been deeply devoted to this project. I am grateful to her beyond language.

I am very appreciative for the comprehensive, excellent, and hard editing work that Wendy Bernstein undertook with skill, patience, and no small amount of goodness.

The onerous task of managing this manuscript from notes and dictation to its book form was artfully undertaken by Mr. Christopher Melton.

This book could not have been written without the goodness and wisdom of my children: Yehuda and Nicole

Poupko, Elisheva and Kevin Schreiber, Chaim and Shoshana Poupko, and Chaya and Aharon Segal, who in the darkest of times were a faithful light.

As in all my learning, my wife, Tzivia Garfinkel, is the one with whom text and idea are ever studied and debated.

Bibliographic Note

In the course of my learning and writing I made use of the various Soncino translations of rabbinic texts, with edits by me. I also made use of several translations from the Koren edition of the Talmud Bavli.

Translations of TaNaKh come from both the standard JPS translation and Robert Alter's excellent translations. In using these translations I occasionally made changes to fit my purpose.

The Hebrew texts of rabbinic literature come from the Bar Ilan database.

The texts from the High Holy Day liturgy are taken from the classic Makhzor, edited by Daniel Goldschmidt.

The translation of the passage from the Zohar is taken from *The Zohar: Pritzker Edition*, translation and commentary by Daniel C. Matt, as is my explanation of it.

The sections that deal with *tefila* and its roots in biblical Hebrew draw on three articles:

"Praying as a Plaintiff," 2011, Shalom E. Holtz.

"Pleading One's Case Before God: A Hittite Analogy for תפלה," 2013, Yitzhaq Feder.

"Psalm 109 and the Legal Meaning of Prayer," 2015, Shalom E. Holtz.

I regularly consulted the Da'at Mikra edition of TaNaKh.

The Story of Chana

1 There was a man from Ramat-haim of the Zuphites, in the hill country of Ephraim, whose name was Elkana son of Jeroham son of Elihu son of Tohu son of Zuph, an Ephraimite.

2 He had two wives, one named Chana and the other Peninna; Peninna had children, but Chana was childless.

3 This man used to go up from his town every year to worship and to give offering to the Lord of Hosts at Shiloh. Hophni and Phinehas, the sons of Eli, were priests of the Lord there.

4 One such day, Elkana brought an offering. Now when he gave portions to Peninna his wife and all her sons and daughters,

5 he would give Chana a single portion equal to theirs, for Chana was the one he loved, though God had closed her womb.

6 Moreover, her rival wife (Peninna) would provoke her (Chana) for the sake of making her (Chana) rage against God, that God had closed her womb.

7 Year after year, as often as Chana went up to the house of God, Peninna would provoke her this way; and Chana would weep and would not eat.

8 Her husband, Elkana, said to her, "Chana, why are you crying and why are you not eating? Why is your heart so tormented? Am I not more devoted to you than ten sons?"

9 After they had eaten and drunk at Shiloh, Chana rose. The priest Eli was sitting on the seat near the doorpost of the temple of the Lord.

10 And she was bitter in life, and she prayed upon the Lord while she wept, yes wept.

11 And she vowed a vow: "O Lord of Hosts, if you will see, yes see, the affliction of your maidservant, and you will bear me in mind, and not forget your maidservant, and will give your maidservant seed of men, then I will give him to the Lord all the days of his life. No razor shall go upon his head!"

12 And it was as she multiplied her praying in the presence and before the Lord that Eli was intently watching her mouth.

13 Now Chana, she was speaking in her heart; only her lips were moving, but her voice could not be heard. So Eli took her for a drunkard.

14 Eli said to her, "How long will you be drunk? Put away your wine from you!"

15 And Chana replied, "No, my lord! A woman hardened of spirit am I. Wine and beer I have not drunk, but I have been pouring out my soul in the presence of the Lord.

16 Do not consider your maidservant a base woman; for it is out of my great anguish and distress that I have been speaking until now."

17 "Then go in peace," said Eli, "and may the God of Israel grant you what you have asked of Him."

18 She answered, "May your handmaid find favor and compassion in your eyes"; and the woman went on her way, and she ate, and her face was no longer [sad] on her.

19 Early the next morning they bowed low before the Lord, and they went back home to Ramah. Elkana knew his wife Chana and the Lord remembered her.

20 Chana conceived, and at the turn of the year bore a son. She named him Shemuel, meaning: I asked the Lord for him.

21 And when the man Elkana and all his household were going up to offer to the Lord the annual sacrifice and his votive sacrifice,

22 Chana did not go up. She said to her husband, "When the child is weaned, I will bring him. For when he has appeared before the Lord, he must remain there for good."

23 Her husband, Elkana, said to her, "Do as you think best. Stay home until you have weaned him. May the Lord fulfill His word." So the woman stayed home and nursed her son until she weaned him.

24 When she had weaned him, she took him up with her, along with three bulls, one ephah of flour, and a jar of wine. And though the boy was still very young, she brought him to the house of the Lord at Shiloh.

25 After slaughtering the bull, they brought the boy to Eli.

26 She said, "Please, my lord! As you live, my lord, I am the woman who stood here beside you and prayed to the Lord.

27 It was for this boy I prayed; and the Lord has granted me what I asked of Him.

28 I, in turn, hereby lend him to the Lord. For as long as he lives he is lent to the Lord." And they bowed low there before the Lord.

Introduction

The drama of Chana (I Shemuel 1,2) is the most important episode in TaNaKh for the Jewish understanding and experience of *tefila*, prayer. Chana, the mother of Shemuel, is for Hazal the primary source in TaNaKh for *tefila* in general and for the unique *tefilot* of the Yamim Nora'im, the Days of Awe, Rosh HaShana and Yom Kippur. The purpose of this work is to review the prayerful career of Chana, and to study her inner life as presented in the text. Understanding her character is the key to appreciating her various *tefilot*, and the unique relationship that she develops with God. This work will describe why, for Hazal, Chana is the richest source of Halakha and Agada to guide the Jewish people in the ways of prayer; and will explain how Hazal use Chana's prayerful life to lend meaning to the unique Rosh HaShana Musaf Amida and Ne'ilah service on Yom Kippur.

The first section will describe the story of Chana in the Book of Shemuel from the perspective of her prayerful relationship with God. The second section will present Hazal's treatment of the person, prayer, and thanksgiving song of Chana. The third section will explain Hazal's application of the Chana drama, person, and song to the *tefilot* and liturgy of the Yamim Nora'im.

The Historical Setting

When and where do we meet Chana and her family? At what point in ancient Israel's history does Chana come forth to get a child of God, to give birth to Shemuel? The drama of Chana, all of two chapters long, is a watershed in the narrative of TaNaKh.

The sacred history of Israel is presented in nine books of TaNaKh. It begins with Be-Reshit, develops through the five books of Moshe, and continues through Joshua, Judges, Shemuel, and Kings. The story begins with Adam and Chava created, placed in the Garden of Eden, and exiled for the sin of hubris. With that rebellion, God loses His partners on earth. The Garden of Eden was designed to be God's earthly residence, shared with Adam and Chava. The loss must be recovered, or all will be awry in the universe. At Sinai, Israel becomes God's new partner, succeeding Adam and Chava. As it says:

שמות פרשת יתרו פרק יט (ה) וְעַתָּה אִם־שָׁמוֹעַ תִּשְׁמְעוּ בְּקֹלִי וּשְׁמַרְתֶּם אֶת־בְּרִיתִי וִהְיִיתֶם לִי סְגֻלָּה מִכָּל־הָעַמִּים כִּי־לִי כָּל־הָאָרֶץ׃ (ו) וְאַתֶּם תִּהְיוּ־לִי מַמְלֶכֶת כֹּהֲנִים וְגוֹי קָדוֹשׁ.

Now then, if you will obey Me faithfully and keep My covenant, you shall be My treasured possession among all the peoples. Indeed, all the earth is Mine, but you shall be to Me a kingdom of priests and a holy nation (Shemot 19:5).

After the union between God and Israel at Mount Sinai, they need — as do all who are married — a residence, a home in which to realize their love and life. Immediately following the covenant, we read:

שמות פרשת תרומה פרק כה (ח) וְעָשׂוּ לִי מִקְדָּשׁ וְשָׁכַנְתִּי בְּתוֹכָם:שמות
פרשת תצוה פרק כט)מה) וְשָׁכַנְתִּי בְּתוֹךְ בְּנֵי יִשְׂרָאֵל וְהָיִיתִי לָהֶם לֵאלֹהִים:
(מו) וְיָדְעוּ כִּי אֲנִי יְקֹוָק אֱלֹהֵיהֶם אֲשֶׁר הוֹצֵאתִי אֹתָם מֵאֶרֶץ מִצְרַיִם לְשָׁכְנִי
בְתוֹכָם אֲנִי יְקֹוָק אֱלֹהֵיהֶם:

And let them make Me a sanctuary that I may dwell among them (Shemot 25:8). I will abide among the Israelites, and I will be their God. And they shall know that I the Lord am their God, who brought them out from the land of Egypt that I might dwell among them, I the Lord their God (Shemot 29:45,46).

The Mishkan, Tabernacle, and ultimately the Beit HaMikdash, Temple, in Jerusalem became the successors to the Garden of Eden. For 40 years, God and Israel journeyed through the desert to the Promised Land. During that time, the Mishkan, situated in the midst of the Camp of Israel, served as their ever-present, portable home. The Tabernacle crossed the Jordan River when God and Israel entered the Land. The Tabernacle was situated in Shiloh, which was both the early capital of the loose union of the Twelve Tribes and the city where God's presence resided. As noted in the opening verses of the Book of Shemuel, the Mishkan of Shiloh served as the place to which all Israel made the pilgrimage to be in God's presence. Not long before the anointment of Sha'ul as king by the prophet Shemuel, the Mishkan of Shiloh was destroyed.

The story of Israel entering the Land appears in the Book of Joshua. At the end of the Book of Kings, the Temple is destroyed and Israel is exiled from the Land as punishment for sin. The culmination of the narrative, when Israel is restored to the Garden during the reign of Cyrus the Persian emperor, is related at the end of Chronicles.

This, in brief, is the basic outline of biblical events. The main premise is the promise made to the patriarchs that their children will be given the Land as the place in which to fulfill the *mitzvot*, commandments, given to them at Sinai. Following a complex and difficult set of circumstances during 40 years in the desert, at the end of the Torah Israel is encamped on the Plains of Moab, poised to cross the Jordan River and enter the Land. In so doing, God will have fulfilled His promise to the Fathers.

The Book of Joshua describes the conquest of the Land and its division among the Tribes. Joshua ends with an affirmation of the *brit*, covenant, in which Israel promises absolute faithfulness to the service of the one God. Joshua dies. The period of Judges follows. The pattern of the book is plain and sad; Israel sins and is punished by subjugation to another nation. God brings a *shofet*, a leader or judge, to save Israel. Israel repents, then backslides and sins. Another oppressor comes, followed by another judge.

This cyclical chaos reaches a crescendo with one of the most horrific episodes in the history of Israel — the case of the Pilegesh B'Giva, Concubine of Giva — which nearly results in the eradication of the Tribe of Benjamin. This episode sets the stage for the narrative of Chana. As a prelude to the saga of Chana, we must listen to the painful description of the Giva story so that we may come to understand the national burden that Chana is destined to relieve. The turmoil of the period of the Judges culminates in the story of the Concubine of Giva. This incident presents the national condition of Israel that Chana, the barren woman, must redeem through her son, Shemuel.

The story begins with a brutal rape by a member of the Tribe of Benjamin. A Levite traveling with his concubine from Bethlehem north to the hill country of Ephraim came into the City of Giva toward evening. The Levite was given hospitality by an old man. In an episode reminiscent of the behavior of Sodom in the Book of Be-Reshit, the locals demanded that the old host surrender the Levite so they can sexually abuse him. The Levite offered his concubine instead. The men of Giva raped her through the night. When the concubine returned, she collapsed at the entrance to the host's house, where her husband had spent the night. The man put her dead body on his donkey. When they arrived home he took a knife, cut the concubine's corpus into 12 parts, and sent one piece to each of the Twelve Tribes of Israel, declaring:

שופטים פרק יט (ל) וְהָיָה כָל־הָרֹאֶה וְאָמַר לֹא־נִהְיְתָה וְלֹא־נִרְאֲתָה כָּזֹאת לְמִיּוֹם עֲלוֹת בְּנֵי־יִשְׂרָאֵל מֵאֶרֶץ מִצְרַיִם עַד הַיּוֹם הַזֶּה שִׂימוּ־לָכֶם עָלֶיהָ עֻצוּ וְדַבֵּרוּ׃

Never has such a thing happened or been seen from the day the Israelites came out of the Land of Egypt to this day. Put your mind to this. Take counsel and decide (Judges 19:30).

The Tribes of Israel assembled — 400,000 fighting men — then demanded that the Tribe of Benjamin surrender the people of Giva who had raped the concubine. The Benjaminites refused, and pressed tens of thousands of men into military service. Initially the Benjaminites were victorious, slaying large numbers of soldiers from the remaining tribes.

The victory of the Benjaminites was short-lived. The army of the eleven tribes launched an all-out assault on the Tribe of Benjamin, putting to the sword their towns, their people, their cattle. In the end, they set fire to the cities, treating the Tribe of Benjamin as if it were a Canaanite city under God's judgment, to be destroyed for the sin of idolatry. In a further assault on Benjamin, the men of Israel swore that no one would give his daughter in marriage to a Benjaminite.

They soon realized the consequence of their oath: The Tribe of Benjamin would become extinct. With no Tribe of Benjamin, the nation, destined to consist of the Twelve Tribes of Israel, cannot constitute itself. Without violating their oath, the men of Israel had to find a way to provide wives for the surviving

Benjaminites. The citizens of another town, Yavesh Gilead, had not been present when the oath was taken. The Israelites dispatched 12,000 warriors and put Yavesh Gilead to the sword. All that remained of the population were 400 virgins, who were brought to Shiloh to marry the men of Benjamin.

Still, there were not enough wives for the men of Benjamin. The text of Judges describes what happens next.

> They said, "The annual feast of the Lord is now being held at Shiloh." (It lies north of Bethel, east of the highway that runs from Bethel to Shechem, and south of Lebonah.) So they instructed the Benjaminites as follows: "Go and lie in wait in the vineyards. As soon as you see the girls of Shiloh coming out to join in the dances, come out from the vineyards; let each of you seize a wife from among the girls of Shiloh, and be off for the land of Benjamin. And if their fathers or brothers come to us to complain, we shall say to them, 'Be generous to them for our sake! We could not provide any of them with a wife on account of the war, and you would have incurred guilt if you yourselves had given them wives.'" The Benjaminites did so. They took to wife, from the dancers whom they carried off, as many as they themselves numbered. Then they went back to their own territory, and rebuilt their towns and settled in them. Thereupon the Israelites dispersed, each to his own tribe and clan; everyone departed for his own territory (Judges 21:19-24).

The Book of Judges closes with the epitaph:

שופטים פרק כא (כה) בַּיָּמִים הָהֵם אֵין מֶלֶךְ בְּיִשְׂרָאֵל אִישׁ הַיָּשָׁר בְּעֵינָיו יַעֲשֶׂה.

In those days there was no king in Israel. Everyone did as they pleased (Judges 21:25).

Where will Israel go from here? The tribal civil war has ended, but the damage to national unity must be repaired. There is no leader on the horizon. At this point Israel has exhausted itself with seemingly no tomorrow. Two distinguished and effective leaders — Moshe and Joshua — united the people and moved them forward to live out the covenantal promises and obligations upon the Land. But with the death of Joshua, chaos ensued again. Despite the central Mishkan in Shilo, all is fractured. The Garden is in disarray. If matters are not put right, Israel will not be able to fulfill its commandments and purposes under the Covenant.

It is in this setting that we first meet Chana and her husband, Elkana. To add to the confusion, we are given notice early in the drama of Chana that all is not well in the Mishkan of Shilo. There is a seemingly inconsequential notice about the family of Eli the High Priest.

שמואל א פרק א ...וְשָׁם שְׁנֵי בְנֵי־עֵלִי חָפְנִי וּפִנְחָס כֹּהֲנִים לַיקוָק.

Hophni and Phinehas, the two sons of Eli, were priests of the Lord there (I Shemuel 1:3).

To appreciate this bit of information it is necessary to distinguish TaNaKh from the modern novel. The modern novel assumes the reader will read the book only once. Therefore, the author knows that the reader brings ignorance to the work. TaNaKh is different: It assumes the reader already knows it when he or she sits down to learn as part of a lifelong pursuit of its meaning. The TaNaKh reader already knows the whole story. It is Shemuel, who is not yet born, who will deliver the prophecy of God's judgment upon the House of Eli. The two sons who should succeed him — Hophni and Phinehas — are corrupt. They will die. The priestly line of Eli will come to a tragic end.

Chana emerges at a time of national unrest. What leadership exists — as exercised by Eli the High Priest — is ineffective and about to end. Neither judge nor prophet appears on the horizon.

As the sixth barren woman of the TaNaKh, Chana's condition is of great national import. Without a child of Sarah, no patriarch would succeed Avraham. If a son were not born to Isaac and Rebecca, there would be no third patriarch named Jacob. Without a child born to Rachel, the Twelve Tribes would not establish the House of Jacob, the House of Israel. The same is true for the episodic barrenness of Leah. The barren wife of Mano'akh must birth a flawed but valiant warrior, Samson, in order to save some of Israel's tribes from the Philistines.

Chana's story is of no less magnitude or consequence. Her barrenness — expressed in her very person — mirrors that of the Twelve Tribes, the ancient Israelite people living in the Land of Israel at the end of the chaotic period of the Judges. Chana emerges following the violent narrative of the Concubine of Giva, whose brutality is unrivaled in TaNaKh. This is barrenness heaped upon barrenness. In that state of utter desolation, we meet Chana and Elkana, deeply faithful to God and each other. Their story contrasts the inhumanity of the concubine story and subsequent unraveling of the bond among the Twelve Tribes.

The barrenness of one woman — Chana — embodies the barrenness afflicting all Israel. The very continuity of the Twelve Tribes as the Nation of Israel is dependent upon the ability of one woman to get with child from the hand of God. Her redemption from barrenness parallels Israel's redemption from chaos. Her child will bring order out of the maelstrom that nearly led to the extinction of Benjamin. The king he anoints will unite the Twelve Tribes into a nation. The personal circumstance of Chana is the stuff of national rebirth.

Chana fits the pattern of narrative in the Torah itself, in which women (e.g., Sarah and Rebecca) are the stewards of transition from one generation's leader to the next. Moments of transition are fraught with danger. The old familiar is lost. The new is yet to be. In the gap between leaders, chaos can ensue. Despite the fact that the critical leadership in TaNaKh is almost always men, women, in many cases, are the custodians of that transition, appointing the next leader. Indeed, it is Batsheva, wife of David, who ensures that Solomon will succeed his father. Where no woman serves as the custodian of leadership transition from one generation to the next — as in the case of No'akh, or the move from Jacob to Joseph, upon the death of Rachel — chaos ensues.

At the end of the period of Judges — after the tragedy of the Tribe of Benjamin, when the current leadership is corrupt — Chana will, through her profound spiritual character and vision, birth and shape the next leader. At Shiloh, itself beset with sin and corruption, Chana will become the only woman in TaNaKh to enter the Mishkan, the Sanctuary.

It was the temptation of Chava that led to exile from and corruption of the Garden. Chana's entry into the Mishkan will restore the Garden. Her son, Shemuel the prophet, will establish the monarchy of the House of David and lead to the union of the Twelve Tribes of Israel as a nation. This will culminate in the construction of the Temple in Jerusalem, the shared home of God and Israel, by Solomon son of David. The long-sought purpose of the Exodus from Egypt will be realized, with God acquiring both partner and permanent home. This is Chana's gift to the Jewish people.

Unlike her predecessors, the five barren women, Chana will have to work exceptionally hard to fulfill her task. Her work will be *avoda shebalev*, the service of the heart — *tefila*, prayer.

According to TaNaKh and to the rabbis, Chana exemplifies the ideal devotional woman and Jew at prayer. She is the *isha hamitpalelet*, the prayerful woman, bar none. Chana is the only person in TaNaKh whose request in prayer is both recorded and granted; and who then returns to God to offer thanksgiving in a *shir,* epic song. Her *tefilot* and *shir*, requests and thanksgiving, make her the most prayerfully active figure in TaNaKh. The life drama of Chana will unfold between initial prayer and culminating epic song, *tefila* and *shir*. The book of Tehilim does present some thanksgiving prayers that are clearly offered to God by a character whose prayers have been answered, but the request and thanksgiving are not woven into a life narrative, as is the case with Chana. She has no rival or parallel in all of TaNaKh or in Hazal.

PART I
The Drama of Chana

1

Chana at Home in Ramah

Before we visit with Chana in Ramah, before we study her saga in prayer, what can we know about her?

Her name tells all, but should we be mindful of Juliet's famous dictum?

> What's in a name? That which we call a rose, by any other name would smell as sweet (*Romeo and Juliet,* II, ii, 1-2).

Juliet is telling Romeo that a name (in their story, their respective family names) is an artificial and meaningless expression unrelated to a person's essence. In TaNaKh, however, Juliet's question has a different answer. What's in a name? Everything — destiny and purpose are found in a name.

The name *Chana* is rooted in and echoes the Hebrew word *khanan,* which expresses beauty, favor, grace, and compassion. The verb form, *lekhanein,* means "to seek compassion through prayer." We know that No'akh found *khein,* favor, in God's eyes; that is to say, when standing in the presence of God, No'akh had the experience that a young child has when her parents' smile washes over her and drenches her with the light of love. The light of the eyes radiates great love. This concept is at the heart of Birkat Kohanim, the Priestly Blessing:

במדבר פרשת נשא פרק ו (כה) יָאֵר יְקֹוָק פָּנָיו אֵלֶיךָ וִיחֻנֶּךָּ.

May God light up His face to you, and ever show you *khein,* loving grace (Numbers 6:25).

It is this *khein*, loving grace and compassion, that prayer pursues in the presence of God. The root word, *khanan,* gives us one of the words for *tefila*, for prayer itself: *Tekhinah* means to have intimate conversation with God, to gain God's loving favor. Chana is, in her person, *tekhinah,* the prayer that seeks grace and compassion from God. Her name echoes compassion, as well as the pursuit of grace and mercy, as in:

שמות פרשת כי תשא פרק לג (יט) וַיֹּאמֶר אֲנִי אַעֲבִיר כָּל־טוּבִי עַל־פָּנֶיךָ
וְקָרָאתִי בְשֵׁם יְקֹוָק לְפָנֶיךָ **וְחַנֹּתִי** אֶת־אֲשֶׁר **אָחֹן**...

And He answered, "I will make all My goodness pass before you, and I will proclaim before you the name Y-H-V-H, and I will be compassionate to whom I am compassionate (Shemot 33:19).

To gain God's *khein*, favor, is to receive the light of His compassion. Chana seeks compassion in intimacy with God. Her name expresses her nature, her destiny, and her life's central activity.

Possessed with the deeper implications of her name, let us visit with Chana. We encounter her in three settings: at her home at Ramah, among the (six) barren women of TaNaKh, and with her family.

Where is home? The story of Chana's life and barrenness begins in Ramah.

שמואל א פרק א (א) וַיְהִי אִישׁ אֶחָד מִן־הָרָמָתַיִם צוֹפִים מֵהַר אֶפְרָיִם וּשְׁמוֹ
אֶלְקָנָה בֶּן־יְרֹחָם בֶּן־אֱלִיהוּא בֶּן־תֹּחוּ בֶן־צוּף אֶפְרָתִי: (ב) וְלוֹ שְׁתֵּי נָשִׁים שֵׁם
אַחַת חַנָּה וְשֵׁם הַשֵּׁנִית פְּנִנָּה וַיְהִי לִפְנִנָּה יְלָדִים וּלְחַנָּה אֵין יְלָדִים:

There was a man from Ramat-haim of the Zuphites, in the hill country of Ephraim, whose name was Elkana son of Jeroham son of Elihu son of Tohu son of Zuph, an Ephraimite. He had two wives, one named Chana and the other Peninna; Peninna had children, but Chana was childless (I Shemuel 1:1, 2).

Chana's prayerful saga is bracketed at beginning and end by mention of Ramah. Nineteen verses after we first meet her, as she concludes her dramatic prayer encounter with God at the Tabernacle in Shiloh, she returns home to Ramah. There in Ramah, God remembers her for the child she so passionately sought of Him.

שמואל א פרק א (יט) וַיַּשְׁכִּמוּ בַבֹּקֶר וַיִּשְׁתַּחֲווּ לִפְנֵי יְקֹוָק וַיָּשֻׁבוּ וַיָּבֹאוּ אֶל־
בֵּיתָם הָרָמָתָה וַיֵּדַע אֶלְקָנָה אֶת־חַנָּה אִשְׁתּוֹ וַיִּזְכְּרֶהָ יְקֹוָק:

Early next morning they bowed low before the Lord, and they went back home to Ramah. Elkana knew his wife Chana and the Lord remembered her (I Shemuel 1:19).

Ramah is no ordinary place. Another barren woman abides there — Rachel, the great love of Jacob. After enduring the pain of childlessness, God remembers her.

בראשית פרשת ויצא פרק ל (כב) וַיִּזְכֹּר אֱלֹהִים אֶת־רָחֵל וַיִּשְׁמַע אֵלֶיהָ
אֱלֹהִים וַיִּפְתַּח אֶת־רַחְמָהּ: (כג) וַתַּהַר וַתֵּלֶד בֵּן וַתֹּאמֶר אָסַף אֱלֹהִים אֶת־
חֶרְפָּתִי: (כד) וַתִּקְרָא אֶת־שְׁמוֹ יוֹסֵף לֵאמֹר יֹסֵף יְקֹוָק לִי בֵּן אַחֵר:

Now God remembered Rachel; God heeded her and opened her womb. She conceived and bore a son, and said, "God has taken away my disgrace." So she named him Joseph, which is to say, "May the Lord add another son for me" (Be-Reshit 30:22-25).

At the very moment when her prayer is answered, Rachel prays for another child. The name of her first son — Yoseif (Joseph) — memorializes her prayer. She asked God, *yosif,* "add another child for me," and He answered her prayer. As she births her second son, Benjamin, she pays for this child with her life.

בראשית פרשת וישלח פרק לה (טז) וַיִּסְעוּ מִבֵּית אֵל וַיְהִי־עוֹד כִּבְרַת־הָאָרֶץ לָבוֹא אֶפְרָתָה וַתֵּלֶד רָחֵל וַתְּקַשׁ בְּלִדְתָּהּ: (יז) וַיְהִי בְהַקְשֹׁתָהּ בְּלִדְתָּהּ וַתֹּאמֶר לָהּ הַמְיַלֶּדֶת אַל־תִּירְאִי כִּי־גַם־זֶה לָךְ בֵּן: (יח) וַיְהִי בְּצֵאת נַפְשָׁהּ כִּי מֵתָה וַתִּקְרָא שְׁמוֹ בֶּן־אוֹנִי וְאָבִיו קָרָא־לוֹ בִנְיָמִין: (יט) וַתָּמָת רָחֵל וַתִּקָּבֵר בְּדֶרֶךְ אֶפְרָתָה הִוא בֵּית לָחֶם: (כ) וַיַּצֵּב יַעֲקֹב מַצֵּבָה עַל־קְבֻרָתָהּ הִוא מַצֶּבֶת קְבֻרַת־רָחֵל עַד־הַיּוֹם:

They set out from Bethel; but when they were still some distance short of Ephrath, Rachel was in childbirth, and she had hard labor. When her labor was at its hardest, the midwife said to her, "Have no fear, for it is another boy for you." But as she breathed her last — for she was dying — she named him Ben-oni; but his father called him Benjamin. Thus Rachel died. She was buried on the road to Ephrath — now Bethlehem. Over her grave Jacob set up a pillar; it is the pillar at Rachel's grave to this day (Be-Reshit 35:16-20).

Where is Rachel buried? Where on the road to Beit Lehem, in the district of Efrat, can we find her? Jeremiah hears her voice and brings us to her resting place.

ירמיהו פרק לא (יד) כֹּה אָמַר יְקֹוָק קוֹל בְּרָמָה נִשְׁמָע נְהִי בְּכִי תַמְרוּרִים רָחֵל מְבַכָּה עַל־בָּנֶיהָ מֵאֲנָה לְהִנָּחֵם עַל־בָּנֶיהָ כִּי אֵינֶנּוּ: (טו) כֹּה אָמַר יְקֹוָק מִנְעִי קוֹלֵךְ מִבֶּכִי וְעֵינַיִךְ מִדִּמְעָה כִּי יֵשׁ שָׂכָר לִפְעֻלָּתֵךְ נְאֻם־יְקֹוָק וְשָׁבוּ מֵאֶרֶץ אוֹיֵב: (טז) וְיֵשׁ־תִּקְוָה לְאַחֲרִיתֵךְ נְאֻם־יְקֹוָק וְשָׁבוּ בָנִים לִגְבוּלָם :

Thus said the Lord: A cry is heard in Ramah — wailing, bitter weeping — Rachel weeping for her children. She refuses to be comforted for her children, who are gone. And the Lord said: Restrain your voice from weeping, your eyes from shedding tears; for there is a reward for your labor. The Lord declared: They shall return from the enemy's land. And there is hope for your future, declares the Lord: Your children shall return to their country (Jeremiah 31:14-16).

Ramah, hallowed by birth and death, is the resting place of the matriarch Rachel. Ramah is the place of Rachel's tears and prayers. The rabbis tell us that God listens to her as He listens to no other, including the patriarchs and Moshe, who also plead for the return of their children from exile.

איכה רבה (בובר) פתיחתא כד מיד נתגללו רחמיו של הקב"ה ואמר בשבילך רחל אני מחזיר את ישראל למקומן.

[Upon hearing the plea of Rachel for the exiled Jewish people] ... instantly the compassion of the Holy One Blessed Be He welled up and He said: In your merit, Rachel, I will restore Israel to their home (Eikha Rabba Proem 24).

Chana, the *isha hamitpalelet,* lives in Ramah, where Rachel died in childbirth, where she prayed for her children, the whole House of Israel exiled. Rachel, whose resting place is Ramah, inspires the prayers of barren women. Ramah is saturated with the tears of mothers for children. Rachel, who shed tears in childlessness and died in childbirth, in the words of Jeremiah, spends eternity praying for all the Children of Israel. In Ramah, Rachel is heard weeping for her children, the whole House of Israel. Chana is molded by her experience. Chana and Rachel are the women of Ramah.

With the assignment of Haftara readings — Chana for the first day of Rosh HaShana and Rachel for the second — the rabbis, in a gesture of peerless curatorial genius, reunite these women of Ramah. They meet once again in the spiritually intoxicated air of Ramah, thick with their tears and prayers of old. The rabbis choose Rosh HaShana, the Creator's birthday, for their reunion. On Rosh HaShana we are summoned to Ramah, home to Rachel and Chana. Later, in the Book of Shemuel, we learn that Ramah is also the home of Chana's son, Shemuel. He never leaves.

שמואל א פרק ז (יז) וּתְשֻׁבָתוֹ הָרָמָתָה כִּי־שָׁם בֵּיתוֹ וְשָׁם שְׁפָטוֹ אֶת־יִשְׂרָאֵל וַיִּבֶן־שָׁם מִזְבֵּחַ לַיקֹוָק.

Then he (Shemuel) would return to Ramah, for his home was there, and there too he would judge Israel. He built an altar there to the Lord (I Shemuel 7:17).

In Ramah, his presence endures long after death.

שמואל א פרק כח (ג) וּשְׁמוּאֵל מֵת וַיִּסְפְּדוּ־לוֹ כָּל־יִשְׂרָאֵל וַיִּקְבְּרֻהוּ בָרָמָה וּבְעִירוֹ.

Now Shemuel had died and all Israel made lament for him; and he was buried in his own town of Ramah (I Shemuel 28:3).

Like Moshe and Aharon, all Israel mourns his passing. Certain biblical narratives and careers have markers at the beginning and end. For Shemuel, Ramah is determinative for his life and spiritual vocation. His parents live in Ramah. He is born in Ramah. He leads Israel and serves God from Ramah. He dies and is buried in Ramah.

Ramah is the place of two of the six barren women of TaNaKh, of whom Sarah is the first and Chana the last. Who are the others?

2

The Barren Women of the Bible

Let us locate Chana in the constellation of women in TaNaKh who are childless — Sarah, Rebecca, Rachel, Leah, and the anonymous wife of Mano'akh (the mother of Samson). The rabbis view them as a group, thus inviting us to understand both the mystery of barrenness and the relationship of these women to each other.

פסיקתא דרב כהנא (מנדלבוים) פיסקא כ רני עקרה שבע עקרות הן,
שרה רבקה רחל ולאה ואשתו של מנוח וחנה וציון.

There are seven uprooted women, Sarah, Rebecca, Rachel, Leah, the wife of Mano'akh, Chana, and Zion (Pesikta de-Rav Kahana 20:1).

"Uprooted" is a more precise and painful translation of *akara*, usually rendered as "barren." Woman as creator of all life, when barren, is uprooted. The place of Zion, personified as a barren woman, will be addressed later. For the moment, we will focus on the six individual women in this passage. These women are unable to realize that first of biblical commandments and blessings: Be fruitful and multiply. This is especially painful because the blessing of fertility and children is God's fundamental assignment and gift to humanity. When God finishes creating life, He assigns that continuing role to the humans just created. At sunset on the sixth day, it is woman and man who must take up that task and obligation. God is faithful to His blessing — so much so that for 20 sinful generations (ten from Adam to No'akh and ten from No'akh to Terakh) no one has any trouble "begetting." They all reproduce with ease and regularity, their sinfulness notwithstanding. The expulsion from the Garden, Cain's killing of Abel, the flood generation, the sin of Ham, the rebellion of the Tower of Babel — this unrelenting flow of sin does not impede the blessing of fertility.

Who is the first woman denied fertility? Who is the first uprooted woman? Who in the very presence of God is childless?

בראשית פרשת נח פרק יא (כט) וַיִּקַּח אַבְרָם וְנָחוֹר לָהֶם נָשִׁים שֵׁם אֵשֶׁת־אַבְרָם שָׂרָי וְשֵׁם אֵשֶׁת־נָחוֹר מִלְכָּה בַּת־הָרָן אֲבִי־מִלְכָּה וַאֲבִי יִסְכָּה: (ל) וַתְּהִי שָׂרַי עֲקָרָה אֵין לָהּ וָלָד:

Avraham and Nahor took to themselves wives, the name of Avraham's wife being Sarah and that of Nahor's wife Milcah, the daughter of Haran, the father of Milcah and Iscah. Now Sarah was barren, she had no child (Be-Reshit 11:29, 30).

Twenty sinful fertile generations, and the first barren woman is the faithful Sarah, the first childless couple Avraham and Sarah. They, the only righteous who believe in God the Creator, are unable to create life.

There is a lesson to be learned from barrenness. Avraham and Sarah will not birth a child until they understand the meaning of their barrenness and the wisdom of birth. Sarah is the first barren woman in the Bible, Chana the last. The first fact we learn about each of these women is that she is barren. In both instances, the text is showing us that barrenness will be the central theme in each of their lives. As the last, Chana's experience and teaching will be the richest and most complex — a repository, an archive of the barrenness of those who preceded her. Chana's story will illuminate that of her predecessors. Among the barren and uprooted, she is the most richly developed character.

To be sure, elements of her life story are found in some of the other childless women of TaNaKh. Like Sarah, Chana has difficult conversations with her husband about barrenness.

Like Sarah, she has to contend with a rival wife who is not infertile. Like Rachel, Chana is deeply pained by her barrenness. This pain is not ameliorated by the love of their husbands.

בראשית פרשת ויצא פרק כט (ל) וַיָּבֹא גַּם אֶל־רָחֵל וַיֶּאֱהַב גַּם־אֶת־רָחֵל מִלֵּאָה...
בראשית פרשת ויצא פרק ל (א) וַתֵּרֶא רָחֵל כִּי לֹא יָלְדָה לְיַעֲקֹב וַתְּקַנֵּא רָחֵל בַּאֲחֹתָהּ וַתֹּאמֶר אֶל־יַעֲקֹב הָבָה־לִּי בָנִים וְאִם־אַיִן מֵתָה אָנֹכִי:

And Jacob cohabited with Rachel also; indeed, he loved Rachel more than Leah... When Rachel saw that she had borne Jacob no children, she became envious of her sister; and Rachel said to Jacob, "Give me children, or I shall die" (Be-Reshit 29:30; 30:1).

שמואל א פרק א (ה) כִּי אֶת־חַנָּה אָהֵב וַיקוָק סָגַר רַחְמָהּ... (ח) וַיֹּאמֶר לָהּ אֶלְקָנָה אִישָׁהּ חַנָּה לָמֶה תִבְכִּי וְלָמֶה לֹא תֹאכְלִי וְלָמֶה יֵרַע לְבָבֵךְ הֲלוֹא אָנֹכִי טוֹב לָךְ מֵעֲשָׂרָה בָּנִים:

... for Chana was the one he loved, though God had closed her womb ... Her husband, Elkana, said to her, "Chana, why are you crying and why aren't you eating? Why is your heart so tormented? Am I not more devoted to you than ten sons?" (I Shemuel 1:5, 8).

Like Rebecca, who inquires of God about matters of fertility and birth, Chana goes to the Mishkan and approaches God. However, Rebecca does so only after she is pregnant. Like the anonymous wife of Mano'akh, mother of Samson, Chana has an encounter with a divine presence about birth and a child. She too has a conversation about matters of child rearing with an agent of the one God, in this case the high priest. Like the wife of Mano'akh, Chana's child will become a *nazir*, a person whose life and being are dedicated to God.

שופטים פרק יג (ג) וַיֵּרָא מַלְאַךְ־יְקֹוָק אֶל־הָאִשָּׁה וַיֹּאמֶר אֵלֶיהָ הִנֵּה־נָא אַתְּ־עֲקָרָה וְלֹא יָלַדְתְּ וְהָרִית וְיָלַדְתְּ בֵּן: (ד) וְעַתָּה הִשָּׁמְרִי נָא וְאַל־תִּשְׁתִּי יַיִן וְשֵׁכָר וְאַל־תֹּאכְלִי כָּל־טָמֵא: (ה) כִּי הִנָּךְ הָרָה וְיֹלַדְתְּ בֵּן וּמוֹרָה לֹא־יַעֲלֶה עַל־רֹאשׁוֹ כִּי־נְזִיר אֱלֹהִים יִהְיֶה הַנַּעַר מִן־הַבָּטֶן...

An angel of the Lord appeared to the woman and said to her, "You are barren and have borne no children; but you shall conceive and bear a son. Now be careful not to drink wine or other intoxicant, or to eat anything unclean. For you are going to conceive and bear a son; let no razor touch his head, for the boy is to be a nazirite to God from the womb on (Judges 13:3-5).

When Sarah and Rachel are barren, they are angry and despairing. We have no hint of Rebecca's inner life, but we do know that Isaac prays for her, while she remains passive. During her episodic barrenness, Leah secures another mate for Jacob to continue to birth the Twelve Tribes. We are told nothing about the life experience of the barren wife of Mano'akh.

The paths of Sarah and Chana diverge. When Avraham is told by God that Sarah will birth him a son, he laughs in disbelief.

בראשית פרשת לך לך פרק יז (טז) וּבֵרַכְתִּי אֹתָהּ וְגַם נָתַתִּי מִמֶּנָּה לְךָ בֵּן וּבֵרַכְתִּיהָ וְהָיְתָה לְגוֹיִם מַלְכֵי עַמִּים מִמֶּנָּה יִהְיוּ: (יז) וַיִּפֹּל אַבְרָהָם עַל־פָּנָיו וַיִּצְחָק וַיֹּאמֶר בְּלִבּוֹ הַלְּבֶן מֵאָה־שָׁנָה יִוָּלֵד וְאִם־שָׂרָה הֲבַת־תִּשְׁעִים שָׁנָה תֵּלֵד:

"I will bless her (Sarah); indeed, I will give you a son by her. I will bless her so that she shall give rise to nations; rulers of peoples shall issue from her." Avraham threw himself on his face and laughed, as he said to himself, "Can a child be born to a man 100 years old, or can Sarah bear a child at 90?" (Be-Reshit 17:16, 17).

When Sarah is told by God that she will birth a son, a successor to Avraham, she too mocks the word of God.

בראשית פרשת וירא פרק יח (יב) וַתִּצְחַק שָׂרָה בְּקִרְבָּהּ לֵאמֹר אַחֲרֵי בְלֹתִי הָיְתָה־לִּי עֶדְנָה וַאדֹנִי זָקֵן: (יג) וַיֹּאמֶר יְקֹוָק אֶל־אַבְרָהָם לָמָּה זֶּה צָחֲקָה שָׂרָה לֵאמֹר הַאַף אֻמְנָם אֵלֵד וַאֲנִי זָקַנְתִּי: (יד) הֲיִפָּלֵא מֵיְקֹוָק דָּבָר לַמּוֹעֵד אָשׁוּב אֵלֶיךָ כָּעֵת חַיָּה וּלְשָׂרָה בֵן:

And Sarah laughed to herself, saying, "Now that I am withered, am I to have enjoyment — with my husband so old?" Then the Lord said to Avraham, "Why did Sarah laugh, saying, 'Shall I in truth bear a child, old as I am?' Is anything too wondrous for the Lord? I will return to you at the time next year, and Sarah shall have a son" (Be-Reshit 18:12-14).

Chana, in contrast, turns to *tefila* when she is first tormented by Peninna, Elkana's other wife. As the subject of Eli's intense gaze, she immerses herself in silence. She stands her spiritual ground against Eli the High Priest, who accuses her of drunkenness when she is in fact praying for a child. Where Sarah laughs, Chana believes. Where Sarah mocks, Chana prays. Where Rachel opposes Jacob, Chana turns to God. Chana is the only one who makes God partner to her pursuit of a child.

What distinguishes Chana from the other barren women? Chana, who brings the very essence of her inner life to God, is understood by no one. Her rival wife torments her. The content of this torment is not recorded; however, it is described with an intense and painful verb. As the text notes, it is with regularity, "Whenever she would go up to the House of God," Peninna would provoke and antagonize her. Her husband thinks the solution lies in eating. Eli declares her a drunk. Each of these three will soon learn a profound lesson from the prayerful life of Chana.

Unlike the previous five barren women, why is it only Chana who is able to intervene with God and, by virtue of her own spiritual resources, gain a child of God? It is not the efforts of Sarah, Rebecca, Rachel, Leah, and the wife of Mano'akh that bring them a child. They birth because of God's unexplained and timely intervention. Chana is the only one of the barren women for whom *tefila* emerges from the heart. It is the unique vocation of Chana to transmute pain and bitterness into insight — an insight that transforms her and shapes a new person before God.

Chana converts pain into belief, bitterness into strength, tears into fortitude. Thus she realizes the national in the individual, and the eternal in the personal. Of the many barren women in this world, Chana is one of the few who discerns the purpose of her barrenness.

Despite the shared experience, no other barren woman in TaNaKh has to work as hard as Chana, through prayer and confrontation with God, to gain a child. Chana is the only one of the six who prays to God for a child — who *negotiates* a child from God. No other biblical figure has as highly developed a prayerful personality and *tefila* experience. No other TaNaKh figure has her person and prayer experience portrayed as visibly and vividly as Chana's.

Knowing Chana's background in Ramah, as well as her place among the six barren women of TaNaKh, we can turn to the immediate life settings that shape her and the drama that unfolds.

3

Family and Tabernacle

The first information we learn about Chana is that she lives in Ramah with her husband, Elkana, and his second wife, Peninna. Soon we learn about this family's activities. Every major figure in TaNaKh inhabits an environment that shapes or expresses his or her life experience. Geography plays a determining role in the religious life drama. Consider both Adam and Chava in the Garden. The Garden of Eden provides for their every need. It is verdant, irrigated, and lush. Its environment is beauty itself, designed to meet the human need for the aesthetic. In the midst of this perfect setting these two, the first humans, want something more. With every need met, they want to be God-like. Israel in the desert confronts the exact opposite situation. There is no water in the desert. There is no green for the eye to see. There is no beauty. Israel is utterly dependent upon God for everything. In that setting they come to experience both the compassion of God, who meets their every need, and the demand of God for just, righteous, and holy living.

The geography of Chana's life centers on prayer and the Mishkan in which it is offered. The Mishkan is not just the place for animal offerings; it is the setting for prayer as well — communal, public, and ceremonial. Such prayer is anything but silent. It is communal, public, and articulated for all to hear. In contrast, Chana's prayer begins in silence. Chana's personality develops in the context of barrenness and the *tefilot* that she offers. As the wife of the pious Elkana, Chana regularly visits the Mishkan in Shilo. Indeed, all the action in the drama of Chana is centered around the Mishkan — within it, traveling to it, planning to travel to it, or leaving it. Shilo is the place, *tefila* is the topography.

Who are the other players in the Chana drama? As is so often the case in TaNaKh, it is family experience that births national saga. Chana's is a family story with profound national consequences. We first meet Elkana and Chana on the way to Shilo. Elkana is clearly a pious man, as expressed in his devotion to God at the Mishkan:

שמואל א פרק א (ג) וְעָלָה הָאִישׁ הַהוּא מֵעִירוֹ מִיָּמִים יָמִימָה לְהִשְׁתַּחֲוֹת וְלִזְבֹּחַ לַיקוָק צְבָאוֹת בְּשִׁלֹה ...

This man used to go up from his town every year to worship and to give offerings to the Lord of Hosts at Shilo ... (I Shemuel 1:3).

Their family experience is Mishkan-centered. Future family events will take place at or in relation to Shilo.

שמואל א פרק א (ד) וַיְהִי הַיּוֹם וַיִּזְבַּח אֶלְקָנָה וְנָתַן לִפְנִנָּה אִשְׁתּוֹ וּלְכָל־בָּנֶיהָ וּבְנוֹתֶיהָ מָנוֹת: (ה) וּלְחַנָּה יִתֵּן מָנָה אַחַת אַפָּיִם כִּי אֶת־חַנָּה אָהֵב וַיקוָק סָגַר רַחְמָהּ:

One such day, Elkana brought an offering. Now when he gave portions to Peninna and her sons he would give Chana a single portion equal to theirs; for Chana was the one he loved, though God had closed her womb (I Shemuel 1:4,5).

Love and barrenness are the contours of Chana's life. Elkana loves her, and God has closed her womb. Her relationship with God develops at the intersection of love and barrenness.

Beyond love, her inner life has another dimension.

שמואל א פרק א (ו) וְכִעֲסַתָּה צָרָתָהּ גַּם־כַּעַס בַּעֲבוּר הַרְּעִמָהּ כִּי־סָגַר יְקוָק בְּעַד רַחְמָהּ:

(ז) וְכֵן יַעֲשֶׂה שָׁנָה בְשָׁנָה מִדֵּי עֲלֹתָהּ בְּבֵית יְקֹוָק כֵּן תַּכְעִסֶנָּה וַתִּבְכֶּה וְלֹא תֹאכַל:

Moreover, her rival wife would provoke her with provocation for the sake of making her rage against God, that God had closed her womb. Year after year, as often as she went up to the house of God, she (Peninna) would do this, and would provoke her this way; and she (Chana) would weep and would not eat (I Shemuel 1:6, 7).

This is no simple nuclear family. It is not just Elkana and Chana who go up to Shilo. Elkana the pious one has another wife, Peninna. Have two wives ever been at ease? Think of Sarah and Hagar or Rachel and Leah. Chana's rival wife provokes her, in hopes that anger will replace Chana's devotion to God and love for Elkana.

The name *Chana* embodies compassion, favor, and prayer — yet she is the target of Peninna, who seeks to alter the spiritual environment of Chana's life. Peninna's campaign goes on for some time; her goal is to keep Chana from praying. One cannot pray from a place of anger. We will soon see that Peninna fails.

As Peninna torments, Chana weeps. She so depletes herself that she is unable to eat. Elkana discerns her heart; he knows that her inner being is in deep suffering. This signals what is to come, for Chana will soon speak to God out of her very heart. Elkana comforts her with thoughtful and loving words.

שמואל א פרק א (ח) וַיֹּאמֶר לָהּ אֶלְקָנָה אִישָׁהּ חַנָּה לָמֶה תִבְכִּי וְלָמֶה לֹא תֹאכְלִי וְלָמֶה יֵרַע לְבָבֵךְ הֲלוֹא אָנֹכִי טוֹב לָךְ מֵעֲשָׂרָה בָּנִים:

Her husband, Elkana, said to her, "Chana, why are you crying and why aren't you eating? Why is your heart so tormented? Am I not more devoted to you than ten sons?" (I Shemuel 1:8).

But Chana continues to despair. Tears, hunger, and bitterness menace her spiritual life. Elkana knows this, for like

Chana he is a person who serves God. He cannot soothe her tears or her bitterness. He cannot give her a child. However, he knows that hunger will only intensify the harsh realities.

The rabbis, however, present a different perspective. They leave no aspect of Chana's life unstudied. Her tears and hunger intrigue them.

מדרש תהלים (בובר) מזמור מב [ג] היתה לי דמעתי לחם. מיכן אתה למד שהצרה משבעה את האדם ואינו מבקש לאכול, וכן אלקנה אמר חנה למה תבכי ולמה לא תאכלי (ש"א =שמואל א'= א ח), מיכן שהבכיה משביע, לכך נאמר היתה לי דמעתי לחם.

My tears have been food day and night (Tehilim 42.4). From this verse you learn that troubles sate a person to the extent that he or she does not seek food. Indeed, this is what Elkana said to Chana. Why do you cry and why do you not eat? (I Shemuel 1:8). From this we know that tears sate and nurture. For it is written: My tears, my tears have been food … (Midrash Tehilim [Buber] 42:3).

When quoting a verse, the rabbis assume the reader knows its context. In turning to Chana to explain how tears nourish and sate the sufferer, they read her into the whole of Tehilim 42. Is not this psalm's description of the lonely and abandoned woman of belief reminiscent of Chana? Is it not possible that they turned to this psalm because it fits as a description of Chana — not just in terms of loneliness, but in the outpouring of the soul and self?

Let's look for Chana in this psalm. Let's look for her in its verses and poetics.

תהלים פרק מב (א) לַמְנַצֵּחַ מַשְׂכִּיל לִבְנֵי־קֹרַח: (ב) כְּאַיָּל תַּעֲרֹג עַל־אֲפִיקֵי־
מָיִם כֵּן נַפְשִׁי תַעֲרֹג אֵלֶיךָ אֱלֹהִים: (ג) צָמְאָה נַפְשִׁי לֵאלֹהִים לְאֵל חָי מָתַי
אָבוֹא וְאֵרָאֶה פְּנֵי אֱלֹהִים: (ד) הָיְתָה־לִּי דִמְעָתִי לֶחֶם יוֹמָם וָלָיְלָה בֶּאֱמֹר אֵלַי
כָּל־הַיּוֹם אַיֵּה אֱלֹהֶיךָ: (ה) אֵלֶּה אֶזְכְּרָה וְאֶשְׁפְּכָה עָלַי נַפְשִׁי כִּי אֶעֱבֹר בַּסָּךְ
אֶדַּדֵּם עַד־בֵּית אֱלֹהִים בְּקוֹל־רִנָּה וְתוֹדָה הָמוֹן חוֹגֵג: (ו) מַה־תִּשְׁתּוֹחֲחִי נַפְשִׁי

וַתֶּהֱמִי עָלָי הוֹחִילִי לֵאלֹהִים כִּי־עוֹד אוֹדֶנּוּ יְשׁוּעוֹת פָּנָיו: (ז) אֱלֹהַי עָלַי נַפְשִׁי
תִשְׁתּוֹחָח עַל־כֵּן אֶזְכָּרְךָ מֵאֶרֶץ יַרְדֵּן וְחֶרְמוֹנִים מֵהַר מִצְעָר: (ח) תְּהוֹם־אֶל־
תְּהוֹם קוֹרֵא לְקוֹל צִנּוֹרֶיךָ כָּל־מִשְׁבָּרֶיךָ וְגַלֶּיךָ עָלַי עָבָרוּ: (ט) יוֹמָם יְצַוֶּה
יְקֹוָק חַסְדּוֹ וּבַלַּיְלָה שִׁירֹה עִמִּי תְּפִלָּה לְאֵל חַיָּי: (י) אוֹמְרָה לְאֵל סַלְעִי
לָמָה שְׁכַחְתָּנִי לָמָּה־קֹדֵר אֵלֵךְ בְּלַחַץ אוֹיֵב: (יא) בְּרֶצַח בְּעַצְמוֹתַי חֵרְפוּנִי
צוֹרְרָי בְּאָמְרָם אֵלַי כָּל־הַיּוֹם אַיֵּה אֱלֹהֶיךָ: (יב) מַה־תִּשְׁתּוֹחֲחִי נַפְשִׁי וּמַה־
תֶּהֱמִי עָלָי הוֹחִילִי לֵאלֹהִים כִּי־עוֹד אוֹדֶנּוּ יְשׁוּעֹת פָּנַי וֵאלֹהָי:

For the leader: a *maskil* of the Korahites. Like a hind crying for water, my soul cries for You, O God; my soul thirsts for God, the living God; O when will I come to appear before God! My tears have been my food day and night; I am ever taunted with, "Where is your God?" **When I think of this, I pour out my soul: how I walked with the crowd, moved with them, the festive throng, to the House of God with joyous shouts of praise.** Why so downcast, my soul, why disquieted within me? Have hope in God; I will yet praise Him for His saving presence. O my God, my soul is downcast; therefore I think of You in this land of Jordan and Hermon, in Mount Mizar, where deep calls to deep in the roar of Your cataracts; all Your breakers and billows have swept over me. By day may the Lord vouchsafe His faithful care, so that at night a song to Him may be with me, a prayer to the God of my life. I say to God, my rock, "Why have You forgotten me, why must I walk in gloom, oppressed by my enemy?" Crushing my bones, my foes revile me, taunting me always with, "Where is your God?" Why so downcast, my soul, why disquieted within me? Have hope in God; I will yet praise Him, my ever-present help, my God (Tehilim 42).

With ease the rabbis see Chana in this psalm. In most citations, the rabbis seek not just alignment between an episode or person and a verse elsewhere in the Hebrew Bible — they also seek association with the larger context of the quoted verse. Chana is compared to the ibex, which is, in TaNaKh, a symbol of both great beauty and abiding loneliness. The ibex is a particular beneficiary of God's caring attention, especially at the moment of birth. She is all alone in the desolate wilderness. Who will midwife her? When God wants to demonstrate to Job that he does not know everything, He challenges him:

איוב פרק לט (א) הֲיָדַעְתָּ עֵת לֶדֶת יַעֲלֵי־סָלַע חֹלֵל אַיָּלוֹת תִּשְׁמֹר: (ב) תִּסְפֹּר יְרָחִים תְּמַלֶּאנָה וְיָדַעְתָּ עֵת לִדְתָּנָה: (ג) תִּכְרַעְנָה יַלְדֵיהֶן תְּפַלַּחְנָה חֶבְלֵיהֶם תְּשַׁלַּחְנָה:

Do you know the season when the mountain ibex give birth? Can you mark the time when the hinds calve? Can you count the months they must complete? Do you know the season they give birth, when they crouch to bring forth their offspring, to deliver their young? (Job 39:1-3).

God, the omnipotent Creator, awesome and mighty, continues to bring forth life long after the six days of creation. He attends to the delicate task of midwifery for the ibex, who is sheltered and hidden in labor by desert colors and cliffs such as those of Ein Gedi. She is precariously perched, alone and seemingly abandoned at the edge of a precipice overlooking an arid desert and canyon. Who will watch over her in the caves and wadis of the Judean Desert as she, all alone, goes into labor? It is God Himself.

The rabbis probe the meaning of Chana's abstinence from food. Starvation is a matter of real and immediate concern for those who love and know the hungered one. That Elkana, her loving husband, is plagued by her condition makes sense, but this concern is not limited to those who love the hungry one. Eating is not just a biological necessity — it is a common human experience that binds people together. Choosing not to eat is a departure from family, friends, and community. Those who choose not to eat threaten their own well-being and seemingly reject those with whom they live. All who fast are deprived of nourishment and community; not all who fast are hungry. Chana, the rabbis teach us, tragically does not feel the hunger. Her tears are bread that fill and satisfy her. Elkana does not fully appreciate that Chana is sated with tears.

Chana ultimately listens to Elkana's words. Restoring herself with food and drink, she is about to embark on a great and complex odyssey through *tefila* into the presence of God. She will soon become the only woman to enter the Mishkan. When she arrives at her destination, Chana will pursue a child through intense conversation — prayer — with God.

At this point we know much about Chana, but precious little about her central life's activity — prayer. The common English-language word and contemporary American usage will be of little help in appreciating Chana's life achievement. What, after all, is prayer?

4

The Jewish Understanding and Practice of Prayer

In order to appreciate this praying woman, a word or two about *tefila* is in order. No other mitzva is quite like *tefila*, the obligation to acknowledge God as Creator and consummate benefactor, the obligation to seek one's needs and the needs of the Jewish people and humanity from God, the obligation to acknowledge that all goodness comes from God. The overwhelming majority of the *mitzvot* are behavioral, fulfilled in deeds and actions. The intent does not much matter, as long as the mitzva is done. If one eats matza on Passover with less than proper or full intent, one has nevertheless fulfilled the mitzva. Not so for *tefila*.

During *tefila*, a person brings the fullness of his or her self into active relationship with the Kadosh Barukh Hu. What does *fullness of the self* mean? The characteristics that distinguish human beings from animals are intellect and emotion, thoughts and feelings. In TaNaKh these features are captured in the *lev*, heart. The heart is the figurative seat of thought and feeling. It is in and through the heart that our intellectual and spiritual selves are integrated, realized, and expressed. The heart symbolizes that which makes us human. God seeks the human who has a portion of the divine intellect. *Tefila*, intimate conversation with the one God, is the way in which the fullness of the human enters into relationship with God.

The rabbis coined a phrase to describe *tefila*: *avoda shebalev*, the service or work of the heart. The idea that one should serve God with a full heart is found in the twice-daily recited Shema. As they pursue the meaning of the Shema, the rabbis turn to Chana's experience to reveal this all-important concept. The Shema is the basic and most exalted of Jewish affirmations. Its central themes are the acceptance of the "yoke of Heaven," the utter unity and singularity of the one God, and the absolute, unconditional love of God. Thus did the Shema become the Jewish martyr's affirmation when choosing death rather than apostasy. The rabbis sought the meaning of the phrase "to serve [God] with the fullness of your heart" in the Shema.

דברים פרשת עקב ראה פרק יא (יג) וְהָיָה אִם־שָׁמֹעַ תִּשְׁמְעוּ אֶל־מִצְוֹתַי אֲשֶׁר אָנֹכִי מְצַוֶּה אֶתְכֶם הַיּוֹם לְאַהֲבָה אֶת־יְקֹוָק אֱלֹהֵיכֶם וּלְעָבְדוֹ בְּכָל־לְבַבְכֶם וּבְכָל־נַפְשְׁכֶם:

If, then, you obey the commandments that I enjoin upon you this day, loving the Lord your God and serving Him with all your heart and all your being (Devarim 11:13).

They teach in a *midrash*:

מדרש שמואל (בובר) פרשה ב [י] וחנה היא מדברת על לבה (ש"א = שמואל א'= א' י"ג). כתיב לאהבה את ה' אלהיכם ולעבדו בכל לבבכם (דברים י"א י"ג), וכי יש עבודה בלב, ואי זו זו תפלה.

"Now Chana, she was speaking in her heart ..." (I Shemuel 1:13). It is written in scripture "... loving the Lord your God and serving Him with all your heart ..." (Devarim 11:13). Is there then service or work of the heart? What is it? This is prayer (Midrash Shemuel [Buber] 2:10).

The question of the *midrash* is based on a simple observation. The Hebrew word *avoda* usually connotes manual labor, occasionally the manual labor of slavery, but may also imply the prohibition against serving idols or alien gods. The rabbis encounter this all-important word in one of the paragraphs of the Shema. They know what manual labor is, and they understand the theatrical and public display of worshipping idols. But what does it mean when the same word is used in reference to the heart? What does it mean "to serve God with all your heart"? This is the inquiry of the *midrash*. *Tefila* is both the work of the heart and the service of the heart.

In this passage, what service or work of the heart is required of the devotional Jew? The rabbis know that a concept will not suffice — a living example is needed so the Jewish people can observe and learn. To find the very essence of prayer — the heart itself — the rabbis probe the Shema; and in pursuit of one of its most important phrases they turn naturally to Chana, the only person of whom it is written that "she was speaking in her heart" during prayer. The service of the heart is Chana's gift to the praying Jew. Her experience teaches that prayer is the work of the whole heart, the very self that an individual brings to God in prayer.

Tefila is the most difficult of *mitzvot*. Unlike gratitude for freedom expressed in the consumption of matza, or the coronation of God through *shofar* sounding, *tefila* allows for no other activity or behavior to express it. It calls upon what makes us humans: the image of God in which we are created, the *tselem elokim*. *Tefila* is performed by that which is at times ambivalent, tempestuous, superficial, impetuous, doubtful, or ignorant. The rabbis recognize the common distractions of our inner lives, and the burden they place on achieving focus and a state of mind fit for prayer.

ברכות דף לא עמוד א תנו רבנן: אין עומדין להתפלל לא מתוך עצבות, ולא מתוך עצלות, ולא מתוך שחוק, ולא מתוך שיחה, ולא מתוך קלות ראש, ולא מתוך דברים בטלים אלא מתוך שמחה של מצוה.

The rabbis taught: **One may neither stand to pray from** an atmosphere of **sorrow nor** an atmosphere of **laziness, nor** an atmosphere of **laughter, nor** an atmosphere of **conversation, nor** an atmosphere of **frivolity, nor** an atmosphere of **purposeless matters. Rather,** one should approach prayer **from** an atmosphere imbued with the **joy of a mitzvah** (Talmud Bavli, Berakhot 31a, Koren Edition).

This roster comprises the distractions normal to the human condition. Prayer requires *kavana*, informed and intentional focus. These diversions stand in the way.

Tefila calls upon the mind and the heart, upon reason and emotion. It requires the same integral characteristics necessary to form a defining relationship. A defining relationship is one without which a person knows not their very self. It is that relationship in which human beings come to know themselves, their destiny and purpose. The individual who seeks relationship brings the fullness of him- or herself to the other. In relationship with God, there is an added degree of difficulty. God is not our equal. *Tefila* takes place *in* and *for* relationship with God.

Prayer is a presumptuous act. Who is the human being — here for but three score and ten, perhaps four — to dare stand before the Almighty Creator, whose being is beyond our conception of oneness and perfection? This relationship requires purity. Purity means that the self a human being brings to *tefila* cannot be encumbered by the vagaries of the human heart.

Let us now return to the heart of Chana.

5

From Husband to God

The last one to whom Chana expressed her inner life before turning to God was Elkana, her husband. She turns from him to God for her prayerful odyssey. Before we explore Chana's prayerful life, let us first enumerate each of the instances when she is at prayer, and the variety of terms employed to describe her practice.

שמואל א פרק א (י) וְהִיא מָרַת נָפֶשׁ וַתִּתְפַּלֵּל עַל־יְקֹוָק וּבָכֹה תִבְכֶּה:

And as for her, she was bitter in life, she prayed to the Lord, while she wept, yes, wept (I Shemuel 1:10).

שמואל א פרק א (יב) וְהָיָה כִּי הִרְבְּתָה לְהִתְפַּלֵּל לִפְנֵי יְקֹוָק וְעֵלִי שֹׁמֵר אֶת־פִּיהָ:

As she kept on praying before the Lord, Eli watched her mouth (I Shemuel 1:12).

שמואל א פרק א (יג) וְחַנָּה הִיא מְדַבֶּרֶת עַל־לִבָּהּ רַק שְׂפָתֶיהָ נָּעוֹת וְקוֹלָהּ לֹא יִשָּׁמֵעַ וַיַּחְשְׁבֶהָ עֵלִי לְשִׁכֹּרָה:

Now Chana was speaking in her heart; only her lips moved, but her voice could not be heard. So Eli thought she was drunk (I Shemuel 1:13).

שמואל א פרק א (טו) וַתַּעַן חַנָּה וַתֹּאמֶר לֹא אֲדֹנִי אִשָּׁה קְשַׁת־רוּחַ אָנֹכִי וְיַיִן וְשֵׁכָר לֹא שָׁתִיתִי וָאֶשְׁפֹּךְ אֶת־נַפְשִׁי לִפְנֵי יְקֹוָק:

And Chana replied, "Oh no, my lord! I am a woman of hardened spirit. I have drunk no wine or other strong drink, but I have been pouring out my heart to the Lord (I Shemuel 1:15).

שמואל א פרק א (טז) אַל־תִּתֵּן אֶת־אֲמָתְךָ לִפְנֵי בַּת־בְּלִיָּעַל כִּי־מֵרֹב שִׂיחִי וְכַעְסִי דִּבַּרְתִּי עַד־הֵנָּה:

Do not consider your maidservant a base woman; for it is out of my great anguish and distress that I have been speaking until now (I Shemuel 1:16).

שמואל א פרק א (יז) וַיַּעַן עֵלִי וַיֹּאמֶר לְכִי לְשָׁלוֹם וֵאלֹהֵי יִשְׂרָאֵל יִתֵּן אֶת־שֵׁלָתֵךְ אֲשֶׁר שָׁאַלְתְּ מֵעִמּוֹ:

"Then go in peace," said Eli, "and may the God of Israel grant you what you have asked of Him" (I Shemuel 1:17).

שמואל א פרק א (כו) וַתֹּאמֶר בִּי אֲדֹנִי חֵי נַפְשְׁךָ אֲדֹנִי אֲנִי הָאִשָּׁה הַנִּצֶּבֶת עִמְּכָה בָּזֶה לְהִתְפַּלֵּל אֶל־יְקֹוָק:

She said, "Please, my lord! As you live, my lord, I am the woman who stood here beside you and prayed to the Lord (I Shemuel 1:26).

שמואל א פרק א (כז) אֶל־הַנַּעַר הַזֶּה הִתְפַּלָּלְתִּי וַיִּתֵּן יְקֹוָק לִי אֶת־שְׁאֵלָתִי אֲשֶׁר שָׁאַלְתִּי מֵעִמּוֹ:

It was for this boy I prayed; and the Lord has granted me what I asked of Him (I Shemuel 1:27).

שמואל א פרק ב (א) וַתִּתְפַּלֵּל חַנָּה וַתֹּאמַר עָלַץ לִבִּי בַּיקֹוָק רָמָה קַרְנִי בַּיקֹוָק רָחַב פִּי עַל־אוֹיְבַי כִּי שָׂמַחְתִּי בִּישׁוּעָתֶךָ:

And Chana prayed: My heart exults in the Lord; I have triumphed through the Lord. I gloat over my enemies; I rejoice in Your deliverance (I Shemuel 2:1).

שמואל א פרק ב (כ) וּבֵרַךְ עֵלִי אֶת־אֶלְקָנָה וְאֶת־אִשְׁתּוֹ וְאָמַר יָשֵׂם יְקֹוָק לְךָ זֶרַע מִן־הָאִשָּׁה הַזֹּאת תַּחַת הַשְּׁאֵלָה אֲשֶׁר שָׁאַל לַיקֹוָק וְהָלְכוּ לִמְקֹמוֹ:

Eli would bless Elkana and his wife, and say, "May the Lord grant you offspring by this woman in place of the loan she made to the Lord." Then they would return home (I Shemuel 2:20).

Ten times the text presents the *tefila* experiences of Chana. As she stands on the terrain of this prayerful geography, Chana encounters God. She converses with God. She requests of God. She bargains and contracts with God. She pours forth her speech to God. She speaks to God in her heart. She converses with God in silence. She prays to God from bitterness and hardened spirit. She does all these upon God, in the presence of God, to God, and from God. This topography of prayer, in which she takes up residence, is all-encompassing. Its landmarks are well known and prominent.

Within so short a passage, so many references are made to Chana's prayer. There is no other figure in TaNaKh whose *avoda shebalev*, service of the heart, is presented in such variety and complexity. In TaNaKh, a book not rich in emotional language, it is noteworthy that Chana's life and relationships are described with uncommon emotional detail. Her rival wife torments. She is hardened. She is not angry. Her husband loves. She is embittered. She speaks silence. She cries. God is silent.

The portrait of Chana is the most emotionally rich of all characters in TaNaKh. By virtue of this, she is the ideal prayerful figure for the rabbis. Her rich inner life is *sha'ar ha'tefila*, the gateway to prayer. Personality and prayer go hand in hand. Chana brings the fullness of her essence to pray her way out of barrenness. She is last of the six barren women of the Bible. As befits a woman who has learned from those who came before, hers is the most intense of experiences. The rabbis take note of the richness of Chana's life and experience.

מדרש שמואל (בובר) פרשה א והיא מרת נפש ותתפלל על ה' ובכה תבכה (שם שם /שמואל א' א'/ י'). כל מעשה חנה בכפלים, כעסה בכפלים, וכעסתה צרתה גם כעס, מנתה בכפלים, ולחנה יתן מנה אחת אפים, בכיתה בכפלים, ובכה תבכה, ראייתה בכפלים, אם ראה תראה, נדרה בכפלים, ותדר נדר.

All the experiences of Chana's life are expressed in doublets: Her provocation is double, *would provoke her with provocation;* her portions are double, *but to Chana he would give a double portion;* her weeping is double, *she prayed to the Lord, weeping and weeping;* her plea for God to see her is double, *if You will see, surely see the suffering;* her vow is double, *and she vowed a vow* (Midrash Shemuel [Buber] Parasha 1).

Five experiences in the narrative of Chana are expressed through the intensifying use of repeated verbs. Chana is so loved that she receives from her husband a double portion. Her provocation, her weeping, her plea, and her vow are all recorded using the emphasis of the doublet.

Before we continue, let's recall where we left off in the drama. Elkana addresses the tears and hunger of Chana. He is in love with Chana. She is the object of his unconditional love. In this love he knows something of her inner life. Perhaps he has a sense of what is about to happen. Is it not possible that he thinks she may now turn to God in her despair? If so, he knows that in order to intercede with God she will need to overcome the exhaustion of fasting. He knows that *tefila* requires physical stamina. It is altogether possible that in calling her to eat and drink Elkana is preparing her for the task ahead. He does this out of love. It is with the love of Elkana that she approaches the Mishkan. Rising above hunger and tears, Chana moves from husband to God and Tabernacle. Prepared for the hard work that awaits her, she enters into the presence of God to offer her plea for a child. She approaches the Mishkan, whose doorway is guarded by Eli. Possessed of conviction and the power of her purpose, though a woman, she is not deterred.

שמואל א פרק א (ט) וַתָּקָם חַנָּה אַחֲרֵי אָכְלָה בְשִׁלֹה וְאַחֲרֵי שָׁתֹה וְעֵלִי הַכֹּהֵן יֹשֵׁב עַל־הַכִּסֵּא עַל־מְזוּזַת הֵיכַל יְקֹוָק:

After they had eaten and drunk at Shiloh, Chana rose. The priest Eli was sitting on the seat near the doorpost of the temple of the Lord (I Shemuel 1:9).

As she draws near, she encounters the formidable presence of the high priest. Rather than standing, he is sitting on the official chair of the one who guards the doorway to the Mishkan. The chair faces the courtyard. Access is limited; not everyone can enter the Sanctuary. With increasing sanctity comes diminishing access.

At the least, this should have made Chana hesitate or ask permission to enter. Not Chana. Eli does not stop her. He cannot stop her. Her entry into the Mishkan is at once normal and surprising. Eli does not stop her, because the geography of Chana's life is the Mishkan, the Sanctuary itself. She is a regular. Perhaps he does not stop her because, looking at her face and her stature, he recognizes a person of uncommon spiritual proportions and determination. Chana's experience of pilgrimage to the Mishkan, of recent hunger, of restoration of body and spirit, makes for a resolute and tenacious religious personality.

The moment of her actual crossing the threshold and entry into the Mishkan is not recorded. Eli is at the threshold and next we find Chana praying in the Sanctuary. Yet Chana is the only woman in TaNaKh who enters the Mishkan. The moment she enters, she comes into the presence of God that she has been seeking. As she prays, her *tefila* lengthens and deepens. She submerges herself in prayer. Eli turns to watch her. Astonished that a woman would enter the Mishkan, he scrutinizes her. He wants to understand the nature of this rare experience — a woman, in the Sanctuary, praying. Not all may stand in the Presence. She has done the work of the heart to gain this place.

Now that we know her location and before Whom she stands, we can study her *tefila* and her experience with God.

6

Personality and Prayer

Chana's prayer is original. It is not found in a *siddur*, prayer book. Her tormented heart is her *siddur*. She will soon speak to God in her heart. No one has ever offered such a prayer; she is unique in that practice. However, she is not unique in the act of spontaneous prayer to and before God. There are many such examples in the TaNaKh. Recall the prayer of Avraham's servant when seeking a wife for Isaac:

בראשית פרשת חיי שרה פרק כד(יב) וַיֹּאמַר יְקֹוָק אֱלֹהֵי אֲדֹנִי אַבְרָהָם
הַקְרֵה־נָא לְפָנַי הַיּוֹם וַעֲשֵׂה־חֶסֶד עִם אֲדֹנִי אַבְרָהָם: (יג) הִנֵּה אָנֹכִי נִצָּב עַל־
עֵין הַמָּיִם וּבְנוֹת אַנְשֵׁי הָעִיר יֹצְאֹת לִשְׁאֹב מָיִם: (יד) וְהָיָה הַנַּעֲרָ אֲשֶׁר אֹמַר
אֵלֶיהָ הַטִּי־נָא כַדֵּךְ וְאֶשְׁתֶּה וְאָמְרָה שְׁתֵה וְגַם־גְּמַלֶּיךָ אַשְׁקֶה אֹתָהּ הֹכַחְתָּ
לְעַבְדְּךָ לְיִצְחָק וּבָהּ אֵדַע כִּי־עָשִׂיתָ חֶסֶד עִם־אֲדֹנִי:

And he said, "O Lord, God of my master Avraham, grant me good fortune this day, and deal graciously with my master Avraham: Here I stand by the spring as the daughters of the townsmen come out to draw water; let the maiden to whom I say, 'Please, lower your jar that I may drink,' and who replies, 'Drink, and I will also water your camels' — let her be the one whom You have decreed for Your servant Isaac. Thereby shall I know that You have dealt graciously with my master" (Be-Reshit 24:12-14).

And the prayer of Jacob, for rescue from his brother, Esau:

בראשית פרשת ויצא וישלח פרק לב (י) וַיֹּאמֶר יַעֲקֹב אֱלֹהֵי אָבִי אַבְרָהָם
וֵאלֹהֵי אָבִי יִצְחָק יְקֹוָק הָאֹמֵר אֵלַי שׁוּב לְאַרְצְךָ וּלְמוֹלַדְתְּךָ וְאֵיטִיבָה עִמָּךְ:
(יא) קָטֹנְתִּי מִכֹּל הַחֲסָדִים וּמִכָּל־הָאֱמֶת אֲשֶׁר עָשִׂיתָ אֶת־עַבְדֶּךָ כִּי בְמַקְלִי
עָבַרְתִּי אֶת־הַיַּרְדֵּן הַזֶּה וְעַתָּה הָיִיתִי לִשְׁנֵי מַחֲנוֹת: (יב) הַצִּילֵנִי נָא מִיַּד אָחִי

מִיַּד עֵשָׂו כִּי־יָרֵא אָנֹכִי אֹתוֹ פֶּן־יָבוֹא וְהִכַּנִי אֵם עַל־בָּנִים: (יג) וְאַתָּה אָמַרְתָּ
הֵיטֵב אֵיטִיב עִמָּךְ וְשַׂמְתִּי אֶת־זַרְעֲךָ כְּחוֹל הַיָּם אֲשֶׁר לֹא־יִסָּפֵר מֵרֹב:

Then Jacob said, "O God of my father Avraham and God of my father Isaac, O Lord, who said to me, 'Return to your native land and I will deal bountifully with you'! I am unworthy of all the kindness that You have so steadfastly shown Your servant: With my staff alone I crossed this Jordan, and now I have become two camps. Deliver me, I pray, from the hand of my brother, from the hand of Esau; else, I fear, he may come and strike me down, mothers and children alike. Yet You have said, 'I will deal bountifully with you and make your offspring as the sands of the sea, which are too numerous to count'" (Genesis 32:10-13).

There is precedent for Chana's prayer offered in the face of barrenness. Isaac prays for his wife, who is childless. She does not pray for herself, and the prayer of Isaac is not recorded.

What is Chana thinking in her heart? What will she say to God? Her prayer is written upon her heart. Only she can offer it. Her experience at the House of God in Shilo begins in torment. She weeps bitterly. Tabernacle and tears — this is the setting of her life. The drama of her personality deepens. She is thoroughly embittered, yet never speaks in anger.

שמואל א פרק א (י) וְהִיא מָרַת נָפֶשׁ וַתִּתְפַּלֵּל עַל־יְקֹוָק וּבָכֹה תִבְכֶּה:

And as for her (Chana) she was bitter of life, she prayed upon the Lord, weeping all the while (I Shemuel 1:10).

The heart from which she prays is bitter with life itself. With just a word or two — *marat nefesh*, bitterness of life, followed by no explanation as one would expect in a contemporary work of fiction — we understand her inner life. TaNaKh, as a work of art, respects its gazing reader. Entrusted with the text, it is expected that the reader will study it and refer to other works of art, such as this *midrash*.

שמות רבה פרשת בא פרשה יט ד"א לב יודע מרת נפשו זו חנה שהרבה היתה מצטערת שנאמר (ש"א =שמואל א'= א) והיא מרת נפש...

The heart knows its own bitterness (Mishlei 14:10). This refers to Chana who was exceedingly pained, as it says: And she was bitter of life … (I Shemuel 1:10) (Midrash Rabba Shemot 19).

In this *midrash*, two juxtaposed verses are reciprocally enlightening. To explain a verse in the Book of Mishlei, the rabbis turn to Chana. She is a portrait of "the heart knows its own bitterness." At the same time, the verse in Mishlei when applied to Chana teaches that only a person's heart knows its bitterness. No other person can presume to know the bitterness of another's heart.

With this same word — *bitterness* — Israel's slave experience is described.

שמות פרשת שמות פרק א (יד) וַיְמָרְרוּ אֶת־חַיֵּיהֶם בַּעֲבֹדָה קָשָׁה בְּחֹמֶר וּבִלְבֵנִים וּבְכָל־עֲבֹדָה בַּשָּׂדֶה אֵת כָּל־עֲבֹדָתָם אֲשֶׁר־עָבְדוּ בָהֶם בְּפָרֶךְ׃

Ruthlessly they made life bitter for them with harsh labor at mortar and bricks and with all sorts of tasks in the field (Shemot 1:14).

This innate bitterness is re-enacted each year at the Passover *seder*.

תלמוד בבלי מסכת פסחים דף קטז עמוד א,ב משנה. רבן גמליאל היה אומר: כל שלא אמרשלשה דברים אלו בפסח לא יצא ידי חובתו. ואלו הן: פסח, מצה, ומרור... מרור על שום שמררו המצריים את חיי אבותינו במצרים, שנאמר וימררו את חייהם וגו'.

R. Gamaliel used to say: Whoever does not make mention of these three things on Passover does not discharge his duty, and these are they: the Passover offering, unleavened bread, and bitter herbs … the bitter herb is [eaten] because the Egyptians embittered the lives of our fathers in Egypt, as it is said, and they made their lives bitter, etc. (Pesakhim 116a, b).

Chana lives the bitterness that Israel experienced in slavery.

The first mention of Chana as a *mitpalelet*, a woman in prayer, notes that, "She prayed upon the Lord, weeping all the while ..." (1 Shemuel 1:10). The brevity of the description only serves to deepen our sense of the magnitude of her prayer. Its length is stated but not described or explained. Detail would only serve to limit her plea in our eyes. "She prayed upon the Lord, weeping all the while ..." drowns us in the enormity of her purpose. Each word within the text summons us to explore worlds of meaning in the life of Chana. Such a personal stance in prayer affects what is spoken to God and how it is presented.

Rabbi Eleazar, who will soon serve as our guide to the *tefila* of Chana and to her relationship with the Kadosh Barukh Hu, describes Chana's presentation to God.

ברכות דף לא עמוד ב ואמר רבי אלעזר: חנה הטיחה דברים כלפי מעלה,
שנאמר: ותתפלל עלֹ ה' מלמד, שהטיחה דברים כלפי מעלה.

Rabbi Eleazar said: Chana spoke confrontationally (literally: "hurled words at the One above") to God, as it says: And Chana prayed upon God. This (*upon* rather than *to*) teaches us that she hurled words at the One above (Berakhot 31b).

Heti'akh, "hurling"! Imagine that — a pious Jew hurling words at God! Rabbi Eleazar bases his statement on the use of the preposition *al*, "upon," rather than *el*, "to." His description of Chana in prayer is supported by the verb "to pray," *le-hitpaleyl*, whose root is *pll*. This is a complex and difficult word. Its various uses and contexts have shaped its meanings and functions. While "prayer" may be the only available word for translating the Hebrew word *tefila*, it is tepid and weak, decidedly inadequate. The definition suffers from being unidimensional, presenting the image of an inferior coming before a superior in order to beg and plead.

Prayer implies speech that moves in only one direction, from the petitioner to the one in power. *Tefila* is rooted in *pll.* A deliberate understanding of this root makes for an appreciation of the complex Hebrew meanings and biblical uses of what is known as prayer. The frequent biblical use of forms of *pll* in legal situations establishes the connection with *tefila*, prayer. Both settings, before the court and before God, involve a person interceding, making a plea for a good judgment at the hands of either the human or divine judge. Thus, *pll* naturally serves as the root of *tefila,* which, in almost all instances, describes the prayer relationship between God and person. *Tefila* takes place in and for the relationship between God and person. *Tefila* is the relationship.

Careful study of the meaning of *pll* and its uses will deepen our understanding of the uniquely Jewish conception of the relationship between God and person.

God is first and foremost Creator and Judge. This role as judge is based on God's purposeful creation. As presented in Be-Reshit, the human created in the image of God is, according to God's plan, the custodian of the natural and social familial order. Hence, it follows that God judges whether or not the human has fulfilled His purpose of maintaining the harmonious order of creation.

Avraham is our first case study in the development of the connection between prayer and courtroom pleading. Avraham is involved in a series of conflicts that call for judicial-like intercession by other people or the divine judge. The first is with his nephew Lot.

בראשית פרשת לך לך פרק יג (ז) וַיְהִי־רִיב בֵּין רֹעֵי מִקְנֵה־אַבְרָם וּבֵין רֹעֵי
מִקְנֵה־לוֹט וְהַכְּנַעֲנִי וְהַפְּרִזִּי אָז יֹשֵׁב בָּאָרֶץ: (ח) וַיֹּאמֶר אַבְרָם אֶל־לוֹט אַל־נָא
תְהִי מְרִיבָה בֵּינִי וּבֵינֶךָ וּבֵין רֹעַי וּבֵין רֹעֶיךָ כִּי־אֲנָשִׁים אַחִים אֲנָחְנוּ: (ט) הֲלֹא

כָּל־הָאָרֶץ לְפָנֶיךָ הִפָּרֶד נָא מֵעָלָי אִם־הַשְּׂמֹאל וְאֵימִנָה וְאִם־הַיָּמִין וְאַשְׂמְאִילָה:

And there was quarreling between the herdsmen of Avraham's cattle and those of Lot's cattle. The Canaanites and Perizzites were then dwelling in the land. Avraham said to Lot, "Let there be no strife between you and me, between my herdsmen and yours, for we are kinsmen. Is not the whole land before you? Let us separate: If you go north, I will go south; and if you go south, I will go north" (Be-Reshit 13:7-9).

In a selfless act of generosity, Avraham mediates the conflict, initiating his career as a judicious and judicial person. God soon presents him with the unconditional grant of land.

בראשית פרשת לך לך פרק טו (ז) וַיֹּאמֶר אֵלָיו אֲנִי יְקֹוָק אֲשֶׁר הוֹצֵאתִיךָ מֵאוּר כַּשְׂדִּים לָתֶת לְךָ אֶת־הָאָרֶץ הַזֹּאת לְרִשְׁתָּהּ: (ח) וַיֹּאמַר אֲדֹנָי יֱקֹוִק בַּמָּה אֵדַע כִּי אִירָשֶׁנָּה:

Then He said to him, "I am the Lord who brought you out from Ur of the Chaldeans to assign this land to you as a possession." And he said, "O Lord God, how shall I know that I am to possess it?" (Be-Reshit 15:7, 8).

Avraham responds not with gratitude or faith. Instead, he asks God, "How do I know that I will possess this land?" This is Avraham's first expression of direct conversation with God about His promises. With this Avraham establishes the precedent that he has standing before God to question His decisions. Avraham establishes here a practice that will stand him in good stead in the future: Just as God is judge of humanity by virtue of creatorship, the human, as custodian of God's creation, has standing to question God's word and promise.

Avraham comes well prepared to stand with God at the overlook of Sodom and Gomorrah. We listen in as God thinks out loud about whether or not to tell Avraham His judgment.

God concludes that He cannot hide this decision from Avraham.

בראשית פרשת וירא פרק יח (יז) וַיקֹוָק אָמָר הַמְכַסֶּה אֲנִי מֵאַבְרָהָם אֲשֶׁר
אֲנִי עֹשֶׂה: (יח) וְאַבְרָהָם הָיוֹ יִהְיֶה לְגוֹי גָּדוֹל וְעָצוּם וְנִבְרְכוּ־בוֹ כֹּל גּוֹיֵי הָאָרֶץ:
(יט) כִּי יְדַעְתִּיו לְמַעַן אֲשֶׁר יְצַוֶּה אֶת־בָּנָיו וְאֶת־בֵּיתוֹ אַחֲרָיו וְשָׁמְרוּ דֶּרֶךְ יְקֹוָק
לַעֲשׂוֹת צְדָקָה וּמִשְׁפָּט לְמַעַן הָבִיא יְקֹוָק עַל־אַבְרָהָם אֵת אֲשֶׁר־דִּבֶּר עָלָיו:

Now the Lord had said, "Shall I hide from Avraham what I am about to do, since Avraham is to become a great and populous nation and all the nations of the earth are to bless themselves by him? For I have known him (by virtue of covenantal obligation), in order that he may instruct his children and his posterity to keep the way of the Lord by doing what is just and right, in order that the Lord may bring about for Avraham what He has promised him" (Be-Reshit 18:17-19).

This is our first indication that someone who practices justice and righteousness has license to intercede with God about His judgments. The one who intervenes or intercedes makes a plea to God. This is one form of prayer, *tefila*. Yet, as we know, Avraham's intercession with God about His judgment on Sodom and Gomorrah is much more than a plea. It is a direct confrontation.

בראשית פרשת וירא פרק יח (כה) חָלִלָה לְּךָ מֵעֲשֹׂת כַּדָּבָר הַזֶּה לְהָמִית צַדִּיק
עִם־רָשָׁע וְהָיָה כַצַּדִּיק כָּרָשָׁע חָלִלָה לָּךְ הֲשֹׁפֵט כָּל־הָאָרֶץ לֹא יַעֲשֶׂה מִשְׁפָּט:

"Far be it from You to do such a thing, to bring death upon the innocent as well as the guilty, so that innocent and guilty fare alike. Far be it from You! Shall not the judge of all the earth deal justly?" (Be-Reshit 18:25).

Will not the God of all the world do justice? This is not a prayer in the conventional sense, but it is *tefila* — intercession with God to alter a decree.

Avraham lives up to God's observation about him. In pursuit of justice and righteousness, Avraham intercedes with

God. Indeed, Avraham's standing with God as a pleader on behalf of humanity is strong enough to cause God to save Avraham's undeserving nephew, Lot, from His judgment upon Sodom and Gomorrah. God must imitate Avraham, who earlier rescued Lot from the fate of war-torn Sodom.

Thus, it follows that God tells Avimelekh, whose estate has been rendered sterile for the sin of kidnapping Sarah, to ask Avraham to intercede for him. Avraham is a *navi*, which in this case means an intercessor, pleader, and advocate. God tells Avimelekh:

בראשית פרשת וירא פרק כ (ז) וְעַתָּה הָשֵׁב אֵשֶׁת־הָאִישׁ כִּי־נָבִיא הוּא
וְיִתְפַּלֵּל בַּעַדְךָ וֶחְיֵה וְאִם־אֵינְךָ מֵשִׁיב דַּע כִּי־מוֹת תָּמוּת אַתָּה וְכָל־אֲשֶׁר־לָךְ׃

Therefore, restore the man's wife — since he is a prophet, he will intercede (*veyitpaleyl*) for you — to save your life. If you fail to restore her, know that you shall die, you and all that are yours" (Be-Reshit 2:7).

This word *veyitpaleyl* commonly refers to prayer and praying. In this verse, to translate it as "prayer" is to diminish the import of the word. God refers Avimelekh to Avraham by virtue of his record of making pleas to God to alter a judgment, as in the case of Sodom and Gomorrah.

It is noteworthy that God gives Avraham a title, a professional designation. God tells Avimelekh that Avraham will intercede for him because Avraham is a *navi*, commonly translated as "prophet." What we have before us is the first use of the word *navi* and the first use of the word *le-hitpaleyl*, "to intercede." Usually we think of a prophet as someone who presents the word of God to people, especially to those who are sinning. Or, the prophet presents prediction and promise of future redemption, per God's instruction. That is why this use of *navi* is so unusual. The initial vocation and responsibility of the *navi* is to engage in *tefila*, "intercession"; to bring the need and word of persons or community to God.

In this first use in the Torah of the word for *praying*, it is employed to describe an intercession, a plea to God to change His judgment. Interceding with God is one form of prayer. Are not some of humanity's most intense and fervent prayers in pursuit of changing God's judgments?

There are two striking features to this. The first is that Avraham, who intercedes to alter a judgment, comes with a well-developed and established record for such intervention. His intercession with God on behalf of Sodom and Gomorrah is the reason that God refers Avimelekh to him. Second, in this first instance of a human interceding with God against a divine judgment, God confirms that this is one of humanity's roles as custodian of justice and righteousness in this world.

The root *pll* presents a family of meanings related to each other: It encompasses and expresses decision, judgment, mediation, and intercession. It lends these meanings and activities to the human approach to God. This relationship and its purposes are expressed in intense and specific ways for which the meanings of *pll* are suited. These definitions develop into the noun form *tefila* and the verb form *le-hitpaleyl. Tefila* takes many forms, including the plain English sense of prayer. In Hebrew, it also expresses intercession with God, the mediation of a great leader or prophet between God and Israel.

Here are some verses and cases that illustrate these various meanings. We have already noted the first two in the life of Avraham.

The first occurrence in the Torah of a form of the word *le-hitpaleyl* is when God tells Avimelekh that Avraham will intercede on his behalf through *tefila*.

בראשית פרשת וירא פרק כ (ז) וְעַתָּה הָשֵׁב אֵשֶׁת־הָאִישׁ כִּי־נָבִיא הוּא
וְיִתְפַּלֵּל בַּעַדְךָ וֶחְיֵה וְאִם־אֵינְךָ מֵשִׁיב דַּע כִּי־מוֹת תָּמוּת אַתָּה וְכָל־אֲשֶׁר־לָךְ׃

Therefore, restore the man's wife — since he is a prophet, he will pray for you — to save your life. If you fail to restore her, know that you shall die, you and all that are yours (Be-Reshit 20:7).

בראשית פרשת וירא פרק כ (יז) וַיִּתְפַּלֵּל אַבְרָהָם אֶל־הָאֱלֹהִים וַיִּרְפָּא
אֱלֹהִים אֶת־אֲבִימֶלֶךְ וְאֶת־אִשְׁתּוֹ וְאַמְהֹתָיו וַיֵּלֵדוּ׃

Avraham then prayed to God, and God healed Avimelekh and his wife and his slave girls, so that they bore children (Be-Reshit 20:17).

In these verses, *ve-yitpaleyl* and *va-yitpaleyl* are normally translated "and he will pray" or "and he prayed." As we have seen, Avraham is interceding to change God's verdict. The next time we encounter the word is at the reunion of Jacob with his long-lost son, Joseph.

בראשית פרשת ויחי פרק מח (יא) וַיֹּאמֶר יִשְׂרָאֵל אֶל־יוֹסֵף רְאֹה פָנֶיךָ לֹא
פִלָּלְתִּי וְהִנֵּה הֶרְאָה אֹתִי אֱלֹהִים גַּם אֶת־זַרְעֶךָ׃

And Israel said to Joseph, "I never judged it possible that I would see you again, and here God has let me see your children as well" (Be-Reshit 48:11).

Here, the root *pll* means that Jacob never judged or estimated it possible that he would again see Joseph.

Another dimension is added to our understanding of this word in the following verse:

שמות פרשת משפטים פרק כא (כב) וְכִי־יִנָּצוּ אֲנָשִׁים וְנָגְפוּ אִשָּׁה הָרָה וְיָצְאוּ
יְלָדֶיהָ וְלֹא יִהְיֶה אָסוֹן עָנוֹשׁ יֵעָנֵשׁ כַּאֲשֶׁר יָשִׁית עָלָיו בַּעַל הָאִשָּׁה וְנָתַן
בִּפְלִלִים׃

When men fight, and one of them pushes a pregnant woman and a miscarriage results, but no other damage ensues, the one responsible shall be fined as the woman's husband may exact from him, the payment to be based on judgment decree (Shemot 21:22).

In this verse, the term is used in association with a judicial proceeding, rendering of verdict, and fulfilling obligation. We next find the word in a setting that any reasonable person might characterize as prayer. There are a number of occasions in the books of Shemot and Bamidbar in which Israel rebels against God and a punishing judgment is forthcoming. When Moshe encounters these judgments, he intercedes. The activity in Bamidbar 11:2 is often translated as "Moshe prayed to the Lord," but this verse is more precisely translated as *va-yitpaleyl,* "and Moshe interceded with the Lord."

במדבר פרשת בהעלותך פרק יא (ב) וַיִּצְעַק הָעָם אֶל־מֹשֶׁה וַיִּתְפַּלֵּל מֹשֶׁה
אֶל־יְקֹוָק וַתִּשְׁקַע הָאֵשׁ:

The people cried out to Moshe. Moshe prayed to the Lord, and the fire died down (Bamidbar 11:2).

Surely Moshe prays, but in this scene he is doing much more. As an advocate on behalf of Israel, Moshe is interceding to alter God's verdict of punishment for Israel's sin. A similar use of the word is found again in Bamidbar 21:7.

במדבר פרשת חקת פרק כא (ז) וַיָּבֹא הָעָם אֶל־מֹשֶׁה וַיֹּאמְרוּ חָטָאנוּ כִּי־
דִבַּרְנוּ בַיקֹוָק וָבָךְ הִתְפַּלֵּל אֶל־יְקֹוָק וְיָסֵר מֵעָלֵינוּ אֶת־הַנָּחָשׁ וַיִּתְפַּלֵּל מֹשֶׁה
בְּעַד הָעָם:

The people came to Moshe and said, "We sinned by speaking against the Lord and against you. Intercede with the Lord to take away the serpents from us!" And Moshe interceded for the people (Bamidbar 21:7).

Israel asks Moshe to intervene with God. They know him to be their powerful advocate. Toward the end of his life, Moshe tells the Jewish people that he interceded on behalf of Aharon.

דברים פרשת עקב פרק ט (כ) וּבְאַהֲרֹן הִתְאַנַּף יְקֹוָק מְאֹד לְהַשְׁמִידוֹ וָאֶתְפַּלֵּל
גַּם־בְּעַד אַהֲרֹן בָּעֵת הַהִוא:

Moreover, the Lord was angry enough with Aharon to have destroyed him; so I also interceded for Aharon at that time (Devarim 9:20).

He then proceeds in the same chapter to remind Israel that he interceded on their behalf as well.

דברים פרשת עקב פרק ט (כו) וָאֶתְפַּלֵּל אֶל־יְקֹוָק וָאֹמַר אֲדֹנָי יְקֹוִק אַל־
תַּשְׁחֵת עַמְּךָ וְנַחֲלָתְךָ אֲשֶׁר פָּדִיתָ בְּגָדְלֶךָ אֲשֶׁר־הוֹצֵאתָ מִמִּצְרַיִם בְּיָד חֲזָקָה:

I interceded with the Lord and said, "O Lord God, do not annihilate Your very own people, whom You redeemed in Your majesty and whom You freed from Egypt with a mighty hand (Devarim 9:26).

That is what it means to be a Jewish leader, to make Israel's case to God. When Israel realizes it is in need of intercession, the people turn to the prophet Shemuel to do so on their behalf.

שמואל א פרק יב (יט) וַיֹּאמְרוּ כָל־הָעָם אֶל־שְׁמוּאֵל הִתְפַּלֵּל בְּעַד־עֲבָדֶיךָ אֶל־
יְקֹוָק אֱלֹהֶיךָ וְאַל־נָמוּת כִּי־יָסַפְנוּ עַל־כָּל־חַטֹּאתֵינוּ רָעָה לִשְׁאֹל לָנוּ מֶלֶךְ:

The people all said to Shemuel, "Intercede for your servants with the Lord your God that we may not die, for we have added to all our sins the wickedness of asking for a king" (I Shemuel 12:19).

When encountering the depth of Israel's sinfulness, God tells Jeremiah:

ירמיהו פרק ז (טז) וְאַתָּה אַל־תִּתְפַּלֵּל בְּעַד־הָעָם הַזֶּה וְאַל־תִּשָּׂא בַעֲדָם רִנָּה
וּתְפִלָּה וְאַל־תִּפְגַּע־בִּי כִּי־אֵינֶנִּי שֹׁמֵעַ אֹתָךְ:

As for you, do not intercede for this people, do not raise a cry of prayer on their behalf, do not plead with Me; for I will not listen to you (Jeremiah 7:16).

In effect, God is telling Jeremiah: Do not intercede with Me on behalf of this sinful people!

In each of these cases, one word — *le-hitpaleyl* — means prayer for the purpose of interceding with God to alter a divine decree, much as one would plead to a judge for a favorable judicial decision.

These several meanings of *pll* are well attested in the Midrash. The rabbis present these understandings — prayer, intercession, and judgment — when commenting upon the action of Pinkhas in the case of Israel's apostasy to the cult of Ba'al Pe'or. Pinkhas is the grandson of Aharon the High Priest. He makes a bold decision to act at a difficult and tragic moment in Israel's history in the desert. At the outset of the 40 years in the desert, Israel committed the terrible Sin of the Golden Calf. Forty years later, Israel is poised to enter the Promised Land. Encountering the Midianite nation near the end of its desert trek to the Promised Land, Israel engages in apostasy, whoring not just after an alien god but with the Midianite daughters as well.

In the midst of this terrible scene, an Israelite man with a Midianite woman in embrace brazenly confronted Moshe in the sight of all Israel. Pinkhas pierces the man and woman with his spear.

במדבר פרשת בלק   פינחס פרק כה (ו) וְהִנֵּה אִישׁ מִבְּנֵי יִשְׂרָאֵל בָּא וַיַּקְרֵב
אֶל־אֶחָיו אֶת־הַמִּדְיָנִית לְעֵינֵי מֹשֶׁה וּלְעֵינֵי כָּל־עֲדַת בְּנֵי־יִשְׂרָאֵל וְהֵמָּה בֹכִים
פֶּתַח אֹהֶל מוֹעֵד׃ (ז) וַיַּרְא פִּינְחָס בֶּן־אֶלְעָזָר בֶּן־אַהֲרֹן הַכֹּהֵן וַיָּקָם מִתּוֹךְ
הָעֵדָה וַיִּקַּח רֹמַח בְּיָדוֹ׃ (ח) וַיָּבֹא אַחַר אִישׁ־יִשְׂרָאֵל אֶל־הַקֻּבָּה וַיִּדְקֹר אֶת־
שְׁנֵיהֶם אֵת אִישׁ יִשְׂרָאֵל וְאֶת־הָאִשָּׁה אֶל־קֳבָתָהּ וַתֵּעָצַר הַמַּגֵּפָה מֵעַל בְּנֵי
יִשְׂרָאֵל׃

Just then one of the Israelites came and brought a Midianite woman over to his companions, in the sight of Moshe and of the whole Israelite community who were weeping at the entrance of the Tent of Meeting. When Phinehas, son of Eleazar son of Aharon the Priest, saw this, he left the assembly and, taking a spear in his hand, he followed the Israelite into the chamber and stabbed both of them, the Israelite and the woman, through the belly. Then the plague against the Israelites was checked (Bamidbar 25:6-8).

God approves of Pinkhas's action. When this episode is recalled in the sacred history that is Tehilim 106, a new word, *va-yefaleyl,* is introduced to describe the event.

תהלים פרק קו (כח) וַיִּצָּמְדוּ לְבַעַל פְּעוֹר וַיֹּאכְלוּ זִבְחֵי מֵתִים: (כט) וַיַּכְעִיסוּ בְּמַעַלְלֵיהֶם וַתִּפְרָץ־בָּם מַגֵּפָה: (ל) וַיַּעֲמֹד פִּינְחָס וַיְפַלֵּל וַתֵּעָצַר הַמַּגֵּפָה: (לא) וַתֵּחָשֶׁב לוֹ לִצְדָקָה לְדֹר וָדֹר עַד־עוֹלָם:

They attached themselves to Ba'al Pe'or, ate sacrifices offered to the dead. They provoked anger by their deeds, and a plague broke out among them. Pinkhas stepped forth and interceded, and the plague ceased. It was reckoned to his merit for all generations, to eternity (Tehilim 106:28-31).

The Talmud takes note of this word. It provides a new way of understanding the Pinkhas episode, as presented in verse 30, above. Rabbi Eleazar, who will be our guide to the prayerful life of Chana, explains the meaning of this new word and idea.

תלמוד בבלי מסכת סנהדרין דף פב עמוד ב ... היינו דכתיב ויעמד פינחס ויפלל, אמר רבי אלעזר: ויתפלל לא נאמר, אלא ויפלל מלמד כביכול שעשה פלילות עם קונו.

And Pinkhas came forward *va-yefaleyl*, and the plague abated ... Rabbi Eleazar said, "It is not written *va-etpaleyl*, rather *va-yefaleyl* ..." This teaches us, if one dare say it, that he engaged in argumentation with his Creator's (God's) judgment [on whether or not justice is done by punishing so many Israelites] (Sanhedrin 82b).

Pinkhas, in the midst of a national crisis, in a grave situation, presents an argument, intercedes to alter God's judgment. In a later *midrash* we learn:

פרקי דרבי אליעזר פרק מו ...קם כדיין גדול ושופט ושפט את ישראל, שנ' ויעמוד פנחס ויפלל מה הלשון הזה ויפלל כדיין גדול, כשם שאתה אומ' ונתן בפלילים.

He (Pinkhas) came forward like a great judge and magistrate and judged Israel. As it says, and Pinkhas came forth *va-yefaleyl*. What is the meaning of this term *va-yefaleyl*? [It means that he judged] like a great judge. As it is written in Shemot, and he shall pay the judgment (Pirkei d'Rabbi Eliezer 46).

These texts demonstrate that, to the rabbis, *va-yitpaleyl*, whose root is *pll*, indicates intercession for the purpose of altering a judgment or gaining a good decree from the court.

The following *midrash* identifies *pll* as one of the ten terms employed in TaNaKh to refer to prayer.

דברים רבה פרשת ואתחנן פרשה ב א"ר יוחנן עשרה לשונות נקראת תפלה ואלו הן, שועה, צעקה, נאקה, רנה, פגיעה, ביצור, קריאה, ניפול, **ופילול**, ותחנונים...

R. Yokhanan said: Prayer is known by the following ten designations: *shaw'ah*, "plea"; *ze'akah*, "outcry"; *ne'akah*, "groan"; *rinnah*, "dirge"; *pegi'ah*, "beseech"; *bizur*, "distress call"; *keri'ah*, "call upon"; *nippul*, "prostration"; *pillul*, "judgment"; and *tahanunim*, "plea for grace and mercy" (Midrash Rabbah Va'etkhanan Devarim 2).

The *midrash* supports each of these terms with a biblical quote (*rinnah*, usually translated as "joyful celebratory prayer," is rendered as "dirge" because of Jeremiah 7:16). There are no exact synonyms. As befits a complex relationship and the many means for its expression, the rabbis compose a list of ten types of prayer, illustrating the inadequacy of any one term to fully capture this complex aspect of the divine–human relationship. The many terms for prayer express well the depth of the human relationship with God.

Pll adds another dimension to the activity and experience of *tefila* that is difficult to translate from Hebrew to English. *Le-*

hitpaleyl is a reflexive verb. In regular verbs, the subject and the object are different, as in *I throw the ball*. In a reflexive verb, the subject and object are the same — *I dress myself*. The action of a reflexive verb is upon or directed to the self, as in *I wash myself. I enjoyed myself.* In Hebrew, the sentence *I dressed myself* is expressed in one word — *hitlabashti*.

Pray cannot be a reflexive verb in English. One prays to God. One offers a prayer to God. The subject is the person performing the action. The direct object is the prayer, which is addressed to God. The action moves in one direction — from the individual to God. In Hebrew, *le-hitpaleyl*, "to pray," is a reflexive verb. Thus, *le-hitpaleyl* describes not a one-directional action in which a person presents a prayer to God, whether praise or plea. Rather, it describes a dynamic action in a relationship characterized by reciprocity and ongoing dialogue.

The Jew who comes before God with intercessory prayer is pleading to alter a judgment or life situation. With this act, the individual is herself seeking to substitute her judgment for God's. She is involved with God in a conversation that draws upon the deepest reserves of the human self. Her prayer activity, which is initially directed to God, is but the beginning of reciprocity. The one who intercedes is engaged in the dynamic activity that characterizes an important relationship between two parties: Each is ever and always affecting the other. Relationships are not static. The Jew at prayer with God is transformed as she seeks change and response from God. As her prayer proceeds to God it then makes its way back to her, as in any deep relationship.

Let us retrace our steps. One of the uses of *pll* is to express intercession with the divine judge. The verb is regularly used in the Torah to describe Moshe's intercession with God. Thus, the use of *pll* naturally develops into what we call *prayer* to God. Is not intercession with God, the supreme judge, quite the same as praying to God? Indeed, for what does one pray to God, if not to alter some life situation or judgment of God's? The human petitioner has standing in the divine court. The human petitioner is not merely pleading or intervening. This intercession in the setting of the divine court is dynamic. It involves the give and take of responding to accusation and judgment. The judge and pleader are involved in an ongoing conversation. Each is affected by this dialectic. Hence, the use of the reflexive verb is necessary to express the movement of words and ideas between and upon the parties. When involved in such a dynamic, two-directional activity, the intercessor is also altering and speaking to the self.

The narrative of Chana in the book of Shemuel provides the most painful presentation of *pll.*

> שמואל א פרק ב (כב) וְעֵלִי זָקֵן מְאֹד וְשָׁמַע אֵת כָּל־אֲשֶׁר יַעֲשׂוּן בָּנָיו לְכָל־
> יִשְׂרָאֵל וְאֵת אֲשֶׁר־יִשְׁכְּבוּן אֶת־הַנָּשִׁים הַצֹּבְאוֹת פֶּתַח אֹהֶל מוֹעֵד:(כג) וַיֹּאמֶר
> לָהֶם לָמָּה תַעֲשׂוּן כַּדְּבָרִים הָאֵלֶּה אֲשֶׁר אָנֹכִי שֹׁמֵעַ אֶת־דִּבְרֵיכֶם רָעִים מֵאֵת
> כָּל־הָעָם אֵלֶּה: (כד) אַל בָּנָי כִּי לוֹא־טוֹבָה הַשְּׁמֻעָה אֲשֶׁר אָנֹכִי שֹׁמֵעַ מַעֲבִרִים
> עַם־יְקֹוָק: (כה) אִם־יֶחֱטָא אִישׁ לְאִישׁ וּפִלְלוֹ אֱלֹהִים וְאִם לַיקֹוָק יֶחֱטָא־אִישׁ
> מִי יִתְפַּלֶּל־לוֹ וְלֹא יִשְׁמְעוּ לְקוֹל אֲבִיהֶם כִּי־חָפֵץ יְקֹוָק לַהֲמִיתָם: (כו) וְהַנַּעַר
> שְׁמוּאֵל הֹלֵךְ וְגָדֵל וָטוֹב גַּם עִם־יְקֹוָק וְגַם עִם־אֲנָשִׁים:

> Now when Eli became exceedingly old he heard about all that his sons were doing to all Israel: how they were lying with the women who were acting as a workforce to the entrance to the Tent of Appointment. He said to them: Why are you acting in accordance with these words that I hear — evil accounts of you from all of these people? Don't, my sons! Indeed, it is no good, the report that I hear God's people spreading. If a man sins against another man, God will intercede for him. But if it is against God that a man sins, who will intercede for him? Yet they did not hearken to their father's voice, for God desired to have them die. But the lad Shemuel went on growing greater and more pleasing, so with God, so with men (I Shemuel 2:22-26).

Let us describe the scene in which this episode is recorded. Shemuel now lives and grows up with God at the Mishkan in Shiloh. His spiritual master is Eli the High Priest. Although Eli will do right by Shemuel, he has failed with his own children, who should rightfully succeed him in the priesthood. They sin something terrible. In these verses, Eli instructs and rebukes them in careful language: If one person sins against another, *u-filelo*, then God can intercede. But if a person sins against God, who will intercede for him?

These verses further enrich our appreciation of the root *pll*. At the opening of the drama, when Eli first meets Chana, he does not recognize that she is engaged in *tefila* that is shaped by the root *pll*, "intercede" or "judge." Chana has judged the situation of her barrenness and, on the basis of that judgment, she intercedes with God.

Eli comes to recognize this dynamic. His understanding of *tefila* as intercession and judgment is expressed in these painful verses. In effect, he is telling his sinning children that, unlike Chana, who advocates for herself with God, no one will intercede on their behalf. The pain increases for Eli as we learn that Shemuel grows up with God. Where Eli succeeded with Shemuel, he failed with his children.

For Rabbi Eleazar, Chana is following in the tradition of Avraham, who confronts God at the overlook of Sodom and Gomorrah, declaring:

בראשית פרשת וירא פרק יח (כה) חָלִלָה לְּךָ מֵעֲשֹׂת כַּדָּבָר הַזֶּה לְהָמִית צַדִּיק
עִם־רָשָׁע וְהָיָה כַצַּדִּיק כָּרָשָׁע חָלִלָה לָּךְ הֲשֹׁפֵט כָּל־הָאָרֶץ לֹא יַעֲשֶׂה מִשְׁפָּט:

Far be it from You to do such a thing, to bring death upon the innocent as well as the guilty, so that innocent and guilty fare alike. Far be it from You! Shall not the judge of all the earth deal justly? (Be-Reshit 18:25).

Or, following in the footsteps of Moshe, who from the outset of his career is quite direct with the Almighty, especially when it comes to the welfare of Israel.

שמות פרשת שמות פרק ה (כב) וַיָּשָׁב מֹשֶׁה אֶל־יְקֹוָק וַיֹּאמַר אֲדֹנָי לָמָה הֲרֵעֹתָה לָעָם הַזֶּה לָמָּה זֶּה שְׁלַחְתָּנִי: (כג) וּמֵאָז בָּאתִי אֶל־פַּרְעֹה לְדַבֵּר בִּשְׁמֶךָ הֵרַע לָעָם הַזֶּה וְהַצֵּל לֹא־הִצַּלְתָּ אֶת־עַמֶּךָ:

Then Moshe returned to the Lord and said, "O Lord, why did You bring harm upon this people? Why did You send me? Ever since I came to Pharaoh to speak in Your name, he has dealt worse with this people; and still You have not delivered Your people" (Shemot 5:22-23).

Like Avraham and Moshe, Chana is able to intercede with God because of her humility and her faithfulness. Avraham can ask for justice only because he believes that God is the judge of all the earth. Note the following verse from Jeremiah:

ירמיהו פרק יב (א) צַדִּיק אַתָּה יְקֹוָק כִּי אָרִיב אֵלֶיךָ אַךְ מִשְׁפָּטִים אֲדַבֵּר אוֹתָךְ מַדּוּעַ דֶּרֶךְ רְשָׁעִים צָלֵחָה שָׁלוּ כָּל־בֹּגְדֵי בָגֶד:

You God are righteous, therefore I will argue with you. Therefore I must summon You to justice. Why does the way of the wicked prosper? Why are the workers of treachery at ease? (Jeremiah 12:1).

Only the one who affirms God's righteousness can summon the Almighty to an account.

7

Bargain, Contract, and Purchase

What is it that Chana will do in conversation with God to gain a child? How will she achieve her goal? Chana does not bring her bitterness to anyone but God. She does not hold her husband responsible for her barrenness, as Rachel does with Jacob. Chana confronts God. At first we can only imagine what she says. Initially, the text does not present the content of her *tefila*. Possibly it is just despair. We know that she is direct with God in her bitterness. Only after she pours forth her desolation to God does she turn to Him with something other than the appeal of a petitioner. She presents her prayer request in a manner not often seen in TaNaKh. She does not merely seek something from God. Rather, in exchange for a request granted, she offers God something in return: If you give me, I will give you. This kind of prayer expresses both judgment and intercession. As she seeks something from God, Chana judges her circumstance and concludes, like others in TaNaKh, that her situation is unjust.

This is surprising. The contemporary person of belief imagines prayer as something brought in offering from an inferior human to the omnipotent and omniscient God. How dare one presume to bargain with the Almighty? Is it not presumptuous to negotiate arrangements with the one God as with a human? Is not the essence of prayer the surrender of the faithful person to the one God?

In the Torah the relationship with God is dynamic, varied, and complex. The mature relationship with God expresses itself in many ways. When falling in love, a person of intellect and integrity surrenders to the object of affection and devotion. This of course has to be reciprocal, otherwise something other than love is at work. In the relationship with the one God, a person of faith surrenders his or her will to the will of God. There are times when a believer gives up his or her very self to God. Yet, at the same time, God has made man and woman partner in the maintenance of creation. That partnership is established by God in the first commandment to the human: Be fruitful and multiply. What God has been doing for six days, God now relies on humans to achieve. The maintenance of nature is not God's responsibility — it is a human responsibility. The creation of family, society, and community is the responsibility of the human. The practice of this partnership creates standing for the human to address God as one would speak with a beloved partner. As God's custodian of creation, nature, and society, the human has not just right but obligation to present the needs of this world, for which we are responsible, to our partner, the Creator. Chana cannot get a child without God. God cannot get a leader of the Jewish people without Chana. Each needs the other.

Listen in on her proposition.

שמואל א פרק א (יא) וַתִּדֹּר נֶדֶר וַתֹּאמַר יְקֹוָק צְבָאוֹת אִם־רָאֹה תִרְאֶה בָּעֳנִי אֲמָתֶךָ וּזְכַרְתַּנִי וְלֹא־תִשְׁכַּח אֶת־אֲמָתֶךָ וְנָתַתָּה לַאֲמָתְךָ זֶרַע אֲנָשִׁים וּנְתַתִּיו לַיקֹוָק כָּל־יְמֵי חַיָּיו וּמוֹרָה לֹא־יַעֲלֶה עַל־רֹאשׁוֹ:

And she vowed a vow: "O Lord of Hosts, if you really will look upon the affliction of your maidservant, and you will bear me in mind, and not forget Your maidservant, and will give your maidservant seed of men, then I will give him to the Lord all the days of his life: No razor shall go up on his head!" (I Shemuel 1:11).

How does Chana come to this bargain? What are the steps she follows to arrive at a contract with God? It is noteworthy that, before she makes her proposal, she secures what she is about to declare. She vouchsafes it with an oath. This is significant: She is not coming as a petitioner or a beggar. She is prepared to guarantee her commitment with a sacred vow.

The sanctity of a vow emerges from the Torah's understanding of language.

Language is the tool of creation. It is the expression of the intellect of God in words. To speak is to imitate the divine. The words of our lips, which give expression to the thoughts of our hearts, both create and destroy. Humans stake their very being on the vows they make, which is why so many oaths in TaNaKh begin with the phrase, "As I live ..." Even God uses the term when making a vow, for example:

במדבר פרשת שלח פרק יד (כא) וְאוּלָם חַי אָנִי

... as I live ... (Bamidbar 14:21).

A vow is the commitment of the self. Once she invokes the oath, Chana makes her declaration. She asks God to acknowledge that she is a tormented person.

God cannot ignore Chana's torment. She asks God to *remember* her. To remember someone is to acknowledge their being and the nature of their life experience. Not to be remembered by God is to live in the dark places where meaningful life does not flourish. She has not been blessed with a child. She cannot be God's partner in creation. This is an ultimate rejection. Without a child, how does she know that she is God's partner? She seeks recognition of her torment. She seeks remembrance from God. She seeks not to be drowned in forgetfulness. This can be realized only through the birth of a child.

Note the steps Chana takes in order to make a contract with God that will result in the birth of a child. First, she secures the contract with an oath. She promises to be faithful to the contract she is about to make. Next, she states what is required of God in order to fulfill the contract. She could have said simply, "If You will give me a child, I will give the child back to You, and thus You will gain the leader and the prophet You need for the next generation." She does not do that. She begins by declaring that there is a prior condition. In order for her to gain a child of God, God must first acknowledge her barrenness and torment. Following that affirmation, Chana requires something else of God: that He remember her and not forget her.

The possibility of God's "forgetfulness" is the stuff of Israel's nightmares.

ישעיהו פרק מט (יד) וַתֹּאמֶר צִיּוֹן עֲזָבַנִי יְקֹוָק וַאדֹנָי שְׁכֵחָנִי:

Zion says, "The Lord has forsaken me, My Lord has forgotten me" (Yeshayahu 49:14).

This is the dark fear of the person of faith, of anyone in a defining relationship — to be ignored by the object of love and attachment, without whom life makes no sense and has no purpose. If such a being forgets them, what remains is the abyss. What does the forgotten seek? God must first move, if one dare say it, from forgetfulness to remembering. God, if one dare say it, can forget. When God forgets a person or people, life and history turn ashen.

Three times in this verse, Chana refers to herself as God's servant. Only one who acknowledges that she is a servant can present *tefila* as Chana does. In *tefila*, humility and brazenness go hand in hand. Only the humble who practice self-denial can be this forward with the Almighty. Often, brazenness is the expression of arrogance, conceit, or anger, but this is not the case with Chana. Her humility is the foundation of her brazenness.

Humility is the mother of truth. It strips away the self-deluding aspects of our lives. It is in humility that Chana comes to know the purpose of her barrenness. The humble Chana gains a deep sense of her purpose and self. Thus, her brazenness is an expression of insight and conviction, innocent of arrogance and hubris. Chana knows what she has learned. Her humility enables her to learn the purpose of her barrenness. This knowledge makes her brazenness pure. Possessed of that knowledge, she comes before God with the brazenness that only humility can present. At the same time, deep piety is at work. What she seeks from God is a son to return to God so that Israel will be led out of its barrenness. As a person of faith, she asks nothing for herself.

What a surprising prayer! Chana presents no mere request — she pursues a deal, a contract with God. She has precedent for this. Jacob, fleeing the murderous designs of his brother, Esau, is homeless, with but Heaven for shelter, rock for pillow, and ground for bed. He is on his way to his mother's family, in the land between the two rivers, in pursuit of refuge and wife. Utterly alone, he turns to God in his abandonment. He does not beg. He does not ask for something. He proposes a deal.

בראשית פרשת תולדות ויצא פרק כח (כ) וַיִּדַּר יַעֲקֹב נֶדֶר לֵאמֹר אִם־יִהְיֶה אֱלֹהִים עִמָּדִי וּשְׁמָרַנִי בַּדֶּרֶךְ הַזֶּה אֲשֶׁר אָנֹכִי הוֹלֵךְ וְנָתַן־לִי לֶחֶם לֶאֱכֹל וּבֶגֶד לִלְבֹּשׁ: (כא) וְשַׁבְתִּי בְשָׁלוֹם אֶל־בֵּית אָבִי וְהָיָה יְקֹוָק לִי לֵאלֹהִים: (כב) וְהָאֶבֶן הַזֹּאת אֲשֶׁר־שַׂמְתִּי מַצֵּבָה יִהְיֶה בֵּית אֱלֹהִים וְכֹל אֲשֶׁר תִּתֶּן־לִי עַשֵּׂר אֲעַשְּׂרֶנּוּ לָךְ:

Jacob then made a vow, saying, "If God remains with me, if He protects me on this journey that I am making, and gives me bread to eat and clothing to wear, and if I return safe to my father's house — the Lord shall be my God. And this stone, which I have set up as a pillar, shall be God's abode; and of all that You give me, I will set aside a tithe for You" (Be-Reshit 28:20-22).

The Midrash compares the vows of Jacob and Chana.

בראשית רבה (תיאודור אלבק) פרשת ויצא פרשה ע [וידר יעקב נדר וגו'] ארבעה הם שנדרו, שנים נדרו והפסידו ושנים נדרו ונשתכרו, ישראל וחנה נשתכרו, יפתח נדר והפסיד, יעקב נדר והפסיד.

And Jacob vowed a vow ... There were four who made vows: Two vowed and lost thereby, and two vowed and profited. Israel and Chana profited;

Yiftakh vowed and lost, Jacob vowed and lost (Midrash Rabbah — Be-Reshit 70:3).

Be careful what you vow! The Midrash is chilling in its description of the high stakes involved in such a pledge. Jacob and Yiftakh each make an oath. They both lose. Yiftakh swore that if God would bring him victory in his battle with the Moabites and the Ammonites, he would offer to God whatever first came forth from his doorway on his return home. His only daughter was the first to greet him and to celebrate his victory. Jacob promised that if God were to restore him in security to his father's household, he would give the Lord a tithe of all his possessions. In the end, he gave up something far more significant than just a tithe. His wife, Rachel, died on the way back to the patriarchal estate, to the Promised Land.

The Midrash then tells us that there were two who profited by their vows.

במדבר פרשת חקת פרק כא (ב) וַיִּדַּר יִשְׂרָאֵל נֶדֶר לַיקֹוָק וַיֹּאמַר אִם־נָתֹן תִּתֵּן אֶת־הָעָם הַזֶּה בְּיָדִי וְהַחֲרַמְתִּי אֶת־עָרֵיהֶם: (ג) וַיִּשְׁמַע יְקֹוָק בְּקוֹל יִשְׂרָאֵל וַיִּתֵּן אֶת־הַכְּנַעֲנִי וַיַּחֲרֵם אֶתְהֶם וְאֶת־עָרֵיהֶם וַיִּקְרָא שֵׁם־הַמָּקוֹם חָרְמָה:

Then Israel made a vow to the Lord and said, "If You deliver this people into our hand, we will proscribe their towns." The Lord heeded Israel's plea and delivered up the Canaanites; and they and their cities were proscribed. So that place was named Hormah (Bamidbar 21:2, 3).

The Israelites made a vow. They promised God that if they were victorious in the battle with the Canaanites of Arad they would lay waste their pagan cities and culture. Israel kept its vow. Israel did not take the spoils of war. The Canaanite cities were laid to waste. Israel was victorious and inherited their land.

Chana also made a vow. Profiting from the commitment to dedicate the as-yet-unborn child to the service of the Lord, she gained a son. What is remarkable is that the two who suffer terrible defeat by their vows are individuals, and the two who profit are the whole nation of Israel and Chana, whose vow moves Israel's history forward. Her life carries within it the weight and destiny of all Israel.

This is no simple task, bargaining with God and making a vow to secure the contract. Only those of significant spiritual stature, who are intimate with the one God and who are regulars in the presence of the one God, can undertake such a bold move to force the hand of God. When they take an oath, Israel and Chana profit by it. Others do not.

A Jew before God is no mere supplicant. Like Jacob, Chana secures her arrangement with an oath. She is prepared to give God something, to barter a son out of God. If God will give her a son, she will give him back to God. She vows that from the womb the child will be dedicated to God's service. She presents this dedication because she has divined the child's life role. The anonymous wife of Mano'akh, the mother of Samson (Shimshon), is instructed by God's agent to make this dedication. She did not dedicate him to God of her own will, as did Chana with her child.

Samson's mother is instructed by God to raise him as a *nazir*. Chana herself proposes that as part of the contract. This demonstrates her high purpose. The dedication of her son to God will be manifest to all. What is a *nazir*? A *nazir* is a person who takes upon himself a vow for a fixed period of time, or a lifetime. In the cases of Shemuel and Shimshon, they don't make a vow; they are designated before birth. The vow prohibits the *nazir* from drinking wine, from cutting his hair, and from contact with the dead. In so pledging, the *nazir* takes upon himself the spiritually elite status of a priest, a man confined to the Temple precincts. He is separated from the ordinary to pursue a life fully with God.

Why does Chana want her child to be a *nazir*? In her pledge, Chana demonstrates that she knows the purpose her child must serve. He will be God's from the womb. Why does she make this vow? Why is she engaged in barter, in deal making, rather than plain, direct *tefila*, petition and prayer? How does she move from silent devotion to articulated vow? The five barren women who precede Chana are either passive or angry. They seem unable to grasp the purpose of barrenness in order to remedy it.

Chana and Sarah are the only two of the six barren women who explicitly acknowledge that they are barren by the will of God. Of Sarah we read:

בראשית פרשת לך לך פרק טז (ב) וַתֹּאמֶר שָׂרַי אֶל־אַבְרָם הִנֵּה־נָא עֲצָרַנִי יְקֹוָק מִלֶּדֶת...

And Sarah said to Avraham, "Look, the Lord has kept me from bearing (Be-Reshit 16:2).

Rachel is admonished by Jacob for not knowing that her barrenness is from God.

בראשית פרשת ויצא פרק ל (א) וַתֵּרֶא רָחֵל כִּי לֹא יָלְדָה לְיַעֲקֹב וַתְּקַנֵּא רָחֵל בַּאֲחֹתָהּ וַתֹּאמֶר אֶל־יַעֲקֹב הָבָה־לִּי בָנִים וְאִם־אַיִן מֵתָה אָנֹכִי: (ב) וַיִּחַר־אַף יַעֲקֹב בְּרָחֵל וַיֹּאמֶר הֲתַחַת אֱלֹהִים אָנֹכִי אֲשֶׁר־מָנַע מִמֵּךְ פְּרִי־בָטֶן:

When Rachel saw that she had borne Jacob no children, she became envious of her sister; and Rachel said to Jacob, "Give me children, or I shall die." Jacob was incensed at Rachel, and said, "Can I take the place of God, who has denied you fruit of the womb?" (Be-Reshit 30:1-2).

Interestingly, neither Sarah nor Rachel prays to God for a child, let alone undertakes the brazen gesture of Chana. Twice in the narrative of Chana we read that God has closed her womb.

שמואל א פרק א (ה) וּלְחַנָּה יִתֵּן מָנָה אַחַת אַפָּיִם כִּי אֶת־חַנָּה אָהֵב וַיקֹוָק סָגַר רַחְמָהּ: (ו) וְכִעֲסַתָּה צָרָתָהּ גַּם־כַּעַס בַּעֲבוּר הַרְּעִמָהּ כִּי־סָגַר יְקֹוָק בְּעַד רַחְמָהּ:

He would give Chana a single portion equal to theirs; for Chana was the one he loved though God had closed her womb. Moreover, her rival wife would provoke her with provocation for the sake of making her rage against God, that God had closed her womb (I Shemuel 1:5, 6).

That Chana is barren by the decision of God is twice stated and twice confirmed. This distinction is not mentioned in the case of Rebecca, Leah, and the anonymous wife of Mano'akh, nor acknowledged by Rachel. The text leaves it to us to infer.

The double notice signals what Chana must do to gain a child. That her plight is the work of God is crucial for understanding her bargain. In the context of Elkana's love for Chana we first learn, "And God has closed her womb" (Shemuel 1:5). The second time we read that God has shut her womb is in the context of Peninna's rivalry, jealousy, and anger (Shemuel 1:6). This is instructive. Her sealed womb gains two reactions: Elkana envelops her in love in response to the despair of barrenness. Her rival wife, Peninna, torments Chana to provoke her rage at God. If Chana rages at God, she will not have the spiritual presence needed to discern why God has closed her womb. Without this insight, she will not be able to contract with God for a child. This will ensure Chana's continued barrenness and Peninna's primacy.

Chana is tested as only the spiritually fit are tested by God. In other literatures, the "gods" torment humans. The TaNaKh human is a majestic figure endowed with the intellect and personality to enter into relationship with God. To gain a child from God, Chana must first realize and then acknowledge that God closed her womb. This awareness makes it possible for her to learn the purpose of God's decision.

Why has God closed her womb? In barrenness lies the promise of birth. She now knows that she will birth only when she acknowledges her child's divine purpose. Her son is born to an assignment from God. He will serve God's will. Chana's contract with God, which is preceded by prayer, works because she knows that it is God who has closed her womb. She knows that the five barren women birthed only when it fit God's plan — when the appointed time arrived for that child to be born in order to assume its divinely destined role. Chana's contract demonstrates to God that she knows her child must be dedicated to the service of God. She is so close to God by virtue of being a praying woman that she comes to know the intent of God. It is not given to her as it was given to the wife of Mano'akh. She has to work for it.

Chana becomes pregnant when she understands that her child must be given to the service of God. When she commits to this, she gains the baby Shemuel. In her silence — her refusal to rage against God's decision — she learns what He seeks from her. Thus, she moves from petition to partnership with God. She is unique even in this exclusive club of the sacred barren. None of them is able to contract with God for the birth of a child. Not one of them, prior to birth, dedicates her as-yet-unborn, prayed-for child to God. The wife of Mano'akh, the mother of Shimshon, does so only when instructed by God. The trial of Chana is testimony to her intellect, her spiritual stature, and her relationship with God.

8

Prayer and the Inner Life

What do we know of Chana's thoughts and feelings, her inner life in the presence of God at Shiloh? The Book of Shemuel portrays the devotional posture of this praying woman and the impression it makes on the observer.

שמואל א פרק א (יב) וְהָיָה כִּי הִרְבְּתָה לְהִתְפַּלֵּל לִפְנֵי יְקֹוָק וְעֵלִי שֹׁמֵר אֶת־פִּיהָ:(יג) וְחַנָּה הִיא מְדַבֶּרֶת עַל־לִבָּהּ רַק שְׂפָתֶיהָ נָּעוֹת וְקוֹלָהּ לֹא יִשָּׁמֵעַ וַיַּחְשְׁבֶהָ עֵלִי לְשִׁכֹּרָה:

As she multiplied her praying in the presence of the Lord, Eli was intently watching her mouth. As for Chana, she was speaking in her heart; only her lips were moving, but her voice could not be heard. So Eli took her for a drunkard (I Shemuel 1:12, 13).

"As she multiplied her praying ..." — as she went on at length — she deepened her *tefila*. It is the depth and length of her silent *tefila* that transfixes Eli's gaze. What does he see? Someone, a woman alone, moving her lips inaudibly in the Sanctuary when nothing else is going on in the Mishkan. Mostly it is the sight of lips moving without words being heard that captures his attention. This suggests something odd, possibly even incoherent on her part. Eli is a spectator, rather than a participant in what is taking place in the Mishkan, which he supervises. Surely he guards the Sanctuary from intruders and from that which is inappropriate. He must now wait and see what this woman is all about. While the high priest is surely conversant in prayer, he is probably not familiar with individual, personal, silent prayer, which apparently was not practiced in the Mishkan. He waits to see the display and hear the prayer language of this brazen woman. He is surprised. Her lips move, but no words come forth for him to hear. She is speaking in her heart and from her heart.

Only God hears the heart. How could a high priest — seemingly a man of prayer — imagine a person in silent prayer to be drunk? Eli is waiting for public, audible worship. He knows that kind of communal prayer from its regular expression in the public square that is the Mishkan. He has never witnessed anyone so intimate with God that she moves beyond words and speech to silence. Eli has no explanation for what he witnesses, so he concludes that she is intoxicated. How ironic that Chana pledges that the child will not drink wine.

Truth be told, the Jew praying to and talking animatedly with the one God — who cannot be seen, heard, or touched — seems like a person alone. How do we react to such a scene? We either fear such people and avoid them, or we get them help. Watching this in his sanctuary, Eli takes her for a drunk.

שמואל א פרק א (יד) וַיֹּאמֶר אֵלֶיהָ עֵלִי עַד־מָתַי תִּשְׁתַּכָּרִין הָסִירִי אֶת־יֵינֵךְ מֵעָלָיִךְ׃

Eli said to her, "How long will you be drunk? Put away your wine from you!" (I Shemuel 1:14).

Eli's rationale is reasonable. It explains and gives him control of something that cannot be tolerated — exceptional behavior in the public Sanctuary.

His assessment of Chana's behavior is grave and ominous. Priests are warned against entry into the Mishkan in a state of intoxication. This is a violation of the sanctity of the place. His first instinct is indictment for sin.

ויקרא פרשת שמיני פרק י (ח) וַיְדַבֵּר יְקֹוָק אֶל־אַהֲרֹן לֵאמֹר: (ט) יַיִן וְשֵׁכָר אַל־תֵּשְׁתְּ אַתָּה וּבָנֶיךָ אִתָּךְ בְּבֹאֲכֶם אֶל־אֹהֶל מוֹעֵד וְלֹא תָמֻתוּ חֻקַּת עוֹלָם לְדֹרֹתֵיכֶם:

And the Lord spoke to Aharon, saying: Drink no wine or other intoxicant, you or your sons, when you enter the Tent of Meeting, that you may not die. This is a law for all time throughout the ages (Vayikra 10:8, 9).

This is painfully ironic. Eli does not recognize that Chana is praying. He accuses her of drunkenness — a grave violation of the Sanctuary. This seemingly drunken prayer of Chana will give the Jewish people the Prophet Shemuel. In his very first prophecy, he will tell Eli that his sons will die for the sin of violating the Sanctuary, the very sin of which Eli accused Chana.

This is the richest and most highly textured portrait of a praying person and of prayerful conduct that we find in TaNaKh. Chana's prayer is lengthy. At some point, all conversation and speech must end or at least pause. How long, after all, can anyone pray to the One who does not respond in speech, who is divinely silent? The person who continues to pray at such length risks much. She may appear to be an exhibitionist, arrogant, unaware of reality, narcissistic. But Chana's *tefila* increases in intensity. Others have different agendas for her. Elkana counsels surrender. Peninna provokes her to storm against God. Eli expects her to pray out loud, as others do. Her silence menaces them all. The more she prays, the quieter her prayer. As the *tefila* increases, she is absorbed by it. She is no longer praying — she is prayer itself. She speaks in her heart, the seat of thought in TaNaKh. Her lips move, but her voice is not heard. Her person is *tefila.* She is prayer.

Look at the personality of Chana in this light. She does not succumb to anger, as did Sarah and Rachel. Peninna is surely filled with enmity because she knows that Elkana loves Chana more than he loves her. She builds a culture of animosity in which Chana never takes up residence. Chana is tested. She responds honestly and plainly. She brings bitterness and tears, but not anger, to the one God. She brings courage — which requires knowing exactly who she is and taking a stand on the ground of her very being. Because Chana does not worship at the altar of anger, because she is deeply aware of her own despair, she is able to stand before the one God and pray.

In its silence, her *tefilot* are known only to God. This is *avoda shebalev*, service of the heart.

> תהלים פרק סה (ב) לְךָ דֻמִיָּה תְהִלָּה אֱלֹהִים בְּצִיּוֹן... (ג) שֹׁמֵעַ תְּפִלָּה עָדֶיךָ כָּל־בָּשָׂר יָבֹאוּ:
>
> For You God who dwells in Zion, silence is prayer ... You hear the prayer of all humanity who come to You (Tehilim 65:2, 3).

We are curious by nature, but the text will not violate Chana's privacy. We are told only what we need to know.

The contrast between Eli the High Priest and Chana could not be more stark. Eli is the descendant of the High Priest Aharon, steward and chief religious official of the Sanctuary at Shiloh, with all of its attendant majesty, authority, and vestments. Chana, barren and despairing, weeping and embittered, bereft of status and lineage, takes her stand on the depth of her spiritual knowledge and the quality of her pious devotion to the one God. Eli is a man of ascribed spiritual status; Chana is a woman of achieved spiritual status. Chana relies on the integrity of her intercession and on the initiative of her vow. That which she so longs for, she is prepared — as a faithful servant — to return to God once her request is fulfilled. What Chana seeks in a child is the opportunity to shape a servant of God. This is the meaning of "... if you will give your maidservant a child, I will give that child to you." Unlike Avraham, who was summoned by God to give his child to God, Chana does so at her own initiative in order to acquire the son.

Chana's response to Eli's accusation is to present her inner life — and this, in turn, teaches Eli the ways of *tefila*. He comes to appreciate that the two are linked: Prayer flows from inner life.

שמואל א פרק א (טו) וַתַּעַן חַנָּה וַתֹּאמֶר לֹא אֲדֹנִי אִשָּׁה קְשַׁת־רוּחַ אָנֹכִי וְיַיִן
וְשֵׁכָר לֹא שָׁתִיתִי וָאֶשְׁפֹּךְ אֶת־נַפְשִׁי לִפְנֵי יְקֹוָק: (טז) אַל־תִּתֵּן אֶת־אֲמָתְךָ לִפְנֵי
בַּת־בְּלִיָּעַל כִּי־מֵרֹב שִׂיחִי וְכַעְסִי דִּבַּרְתִּי עַד־הֵנָּה:

And Chana replied, "No, my lord! A woman hardened of spirit am I. Wine and beer I have not drunk, but I have been pouring out my soul in the presence of the Lord. Do not consider your maidservant a base woman; for it is out of my great anguish and distress that I have been speaking until now" (I Shemuel 1:15, 16).

Chana is such an emotionally textured and sophisticated personality that she summarizes her thoughts and feelings, her soul's life, in but a few words. She stands her ground. Eli realizes his error; she is not drunk. She is a woman "of hardened and bitter spirit." She brings this spiritual knowledge of self to the Mishkan. When Eli confronts her, Chana tells him that she is standing, that her prayer is *lifnei Hashem*, in the face of the presence of God. That phrase is repeated twice. She is standing in the Mishkan. As such, she is *lifnei*, in the presence of the one God. Not all may stand in the presence. She has done the work of the heart to gain this place. Her spiritual geography is now clear. She is in the space of the Mishkan by virtue of moving from anger to deep self-insight. She is standing in the presence by virtue of her heart's work. Now we can study her *tefila*.

9
Outpouring of the Spirit

What is she doing in the presence? Barrenness and torment have driven her to this outpouring. Accused of pouring wine into herself to the point of drunkenness, Chana retorts: No, I have poured no drink for myself or into myself. I have poured out my self to God.

What a biting sense of humor! She pours out her very life before and to God.

This is what it means to be a praying person: to pour out, to empty one's being before God. This is the remarkable self-portrait that Chana presents. Previously, the narrator has described her stance in *tefila*. Now, in response to the accusation of drunkenness, she presents her inner life to Eli the High Priest.

Eli is unschooled in the ways of silence, and also in the relational intimacy between persons and between God and person. It is relationship that God seeks with the human. God's first words are in pursuit of such connection when He calls out to Adam and Chava, "Where are you?" The ways of relationship require the outpouring of self, one to the other. Where there is no outpouring of self, there is nothing but superficiality.

Chana's purpose is to explain herself and to teach Eli the ways of prayer. She appears drunk because she is emptying herself. Like a drunk, she seems not to reserve the private. She exposes all. She explains her purpose with one verb —*va-eshpokh*, "and I poured out." What did she pour out? Her life, her being. Because she risks exhibitionism with the outpouring of her soul, she remains in silence. Her outpouring is known only to God.

Chana teaches Eli the High Priest the nature of *tefila*. Later in TaNaKh we will see similar uses of *va-eshpokh* to describe the ideal and intense experience of standing before God in *tefila* — but Chana is the only figure in TaNaKh to pour out her very person to God. What does it mean to pour forth one's very being? The imagery is clear: to empty oneself as one would a pitcher of water, to thoroughly expose and present oneself to God, to leave nothing hidden, to reserve nothing for the self, to place one's being in the hands of God.

The next time we encounter such an "outpouring" experience is in the Book of Yo'el:

יואל פרק ג (א) וְהָיָה אַחֲרֵי־כֵן אֶשְׁפּוֹךְ אֶת־רוּחִי עַל־כָּל־בָּשָׂר וְנִבְּאוּ בְּנֵיכֶם וּבְנוֹתֵיכֶם זִקְנֵיכֶם חֲלֹמוֹת יַחֲלֹמוּן בַּחוּרֵיכֶם חֶזְיֹנוֹת יִרְאוּ: (ב) וְגַם עַל־הָעֲבָדִים וְעַל־הַשְּׁפָחוֹת בַּיָּמִים הָהֵמָּה אֶשְׁפּוֹךְ אֶת־רוּחִי:

After that, I will pour out My spirit on all flesh; your sons and daughters shall prophesy; your old men shall dream dreams, and your young men shall see visions. I will even pour out My spirit upon male and female servants in those days (Yo'el 3:1, 2).

In the End of Days, God promises that Jewish sons and daughters, old people and young people, even those in the lowest socio-economic class, will prophesy, will be filled with ecstasy. God promises to pour out His spirit upon them, into them. Chana and God are the only two in TaNaKh who "pour out" their selves or spirits.

In the Book of Tehilim, we have several uses of this expression.

תהלים פרק מב (א) לַמְנַצֵּחַ מַשְׂכִּיל לִבְנֵי־קֹרַח: (ב) כְּאַיָּל תַּעֲרֹג עַל־אֲפִיקֵי־מָיִם כֵּן נַפְשִׁי תַעֲרֹג אֵלֶיךָ אֱלֹהִים: (ג) צָמְאָה נַפְשִׁי לֵאלֹהִים לְאֵל חָי מָתַי אָבוֹא וְאֵרָאֶה פְּנֵי אֱלֹהִים: (ד) הָיְתָה־לִּי דִמְעָתִי לֶחֶם יוֹמָם וָלָיְלָה בֶּאֱמֹר אֵלַי כָּל־הַיּוֹם אַיֵּה אֱלֹהֶיךָ: (ה) אֵלֶּה אֶזְכְּרָה וְאֶשְׁפְּכָה עָלַי נַפְשִׁי כִּי אֶעֱבֹר בַּסָּךְ אֶדַּדֵּם עַד־בֵּית אֱלֹהִים בְּקוֹל־רִנָּה וְתוֹדָה הָמוֹן חוֹגֵג:

For the leader. A *maskil* of the Korahites. Like a hind crying for water, my soul cries for You, O God; my soul thirsts for God, the living God; O when will I come to appear before God! My tears have been my food day and night; I am ever taunted with, "Where is your God?" When I think of this, I pour out my being: how I walked with the crowd, moved with them, the festive throng, to the House of God with joyous shouts of praise (Tehilim 42:1-5).

This passage expresses a tremendous longing, an unquenchable thirst, to be in the presence of the one God. This is a thirst like that of the ibex in the wilderness crying for water over arid wadis. The one who longs for God pours out her being in pursuit of God, especially when she recalls being in His presence with the Jewish people in the Temple.

Silence and outpouring of self are linked.

תהלים פרק סב (ו) אַךְ לֵאלֹהִים דּוֹמִּי נַפְשִׁי כִּי־מִמֶּנּוּ תִּקְוָתִי: (ז) אַךְ־הוּא צוּרִי וִישׁוּעָתִי מִשְׂגַּבִּי לֹא אֶמּוֹט: (ח) עַל־אֱלֹהִים יִשְׁעִי וּכְבוֹדִי צוּר־עֻזִּי מַחְסִי בֵּאלֹהִים: (ט) בִּטְחוּ בוֹ בְכָל־עֵת עָם שִׁפְכוּ־לְפָנָיו לְבַבְכֶם אֱלֹהִים מַחֲסֶה־לָּנוּ סֶלָה:

Only for God is my very being still, for my hope comes from Him. He is my rock and deliverance, my haven; I shall not be shaken. I rely on God, my deliverance and glory, my rock of strength; in God is my refuge. Trust in Him at all times, O people; pour out your hearts before Him; God is our refuge. *Selah* (Tehilim 62:6-9).

Like Chana, the psalmist knows that through silence the *mitpalelet* reaches the stage of outpouring, of emptying the self before the Kadosh Barukh Hu. The noisy person is too focused on hearing the self to empty herself to God.

The psalmist calls upon the Jewish people to pour out their hearts before God in an act of full trust. Without such trust, outpouring of the soul is dangerous. Based on his experience of trusting in God, he turns to the ancient Jewish people and says, in effect: You can deposit your very self with God. You can place everything of yourself before Him; pour out your heart to Him, for God is our protector and shelter.

Growing faint, with focus on the inner life, brings the prayerful person to this outpouring.

תהלים פרק קב (א) תְּפִלָּה לְעָנִי כִי־יַעֲטֹף וְלִפְנֵי יְקֹוָק יִשְׁפֹּךְ שִׂיחוֹ (ב) יְקֹוָק שִׁמְעָה תְפִלָּתִי וְשַׁוְעָתִי אֵלֶיךָ תָבוֹא: (ג) אַל־תַּסְתֵּר פָּנֶיךָ מִמֶּנִּי בְּיוֹם צַר לִי הַטֵּה־אֵלַי אָזְנֶךָ בְּיוֹם אֶקְרָא מַהֵר עֲנֵנִי:

A prayer of the tormented man when he is faint and pours forth his plea before the Lord. O Lord, hear my prayer; let my cry come before You. Do not hide Your face from me in my time of trouble; turn Your ear to me; when I cry, answer me speedily (Tehilim 102:1-3).

This is the prayer of a person so exhausted from torment that he is faint. He is desperate that God not hide His face from him in his day of trouble and pain. It is at this moment that he pours forth his prayer before God. The rabbis used this verse to illustrate the prayer of Isaac as he stood all alone in the field at sunset.

בראשית רבה פרשת חיי שרה פרשה ס ויצא יצחק לשוח בשדה לפנות ערב ואין שיחה אלא תפילה תפילה לעני כי יעטף ולפני י"י ישפך שיחו (תהלים קב:א) ...

And Isaac went out *lasu'akh* in the field toward evening ... (Be-Reshit 24:63). By *lasu'akh*, prayer is meant, as it says: A prayer of the tormented when he is faint, and pours out his *si'akh*, prayer, before the Lord (Tehilim 102:1) ... (Midrash Rabba Be-Reshit 60).

That pouring out one's being to God is a feature of *tefila* at its most intimate is well documented in the Book of Tehilim, but it is expressed in the prayer life of only one person in TaNaKh — Chana.

Mark the path that Chana walks through the stages of her various prayers and presentations to God. She is, first of all, a regular who makes the pilgrimage to bring *korbanot*, animal offerings. At the most festive of times in the sacred calendar, the Pilgrimage Festivals, in this service of God she suffers the taunting of Peninna. Unlike Rachel, who in her barrenness despises her rival wife and sister, Leah, Chana responds to torment in silence. Sunken in silence, she is unable to eat and drink. With the love of Elkana she restores herself. Then, with one verb she begins her resolute path — *vatakam,* "she stood up." This one word is dense with action and meaning. She stood up and came forth and walked and entered.

שמואל א פרק א (ט) וַתָּקָם חַנָּה אַחֲרֵי אָכְלָה בְשִׁלֹה וְאַחֲרֵי שָׁתֹה וְעֵלִי הַכֹּהֵן
יֹשֵׁב עַל־הַכִּסֵּא עַל־מְזוּזַת הֵיכַל יְקֹוָק: (י) וְהִיא מָרַת נָפֶשׁ וַתִּתְפַּלֵּל עַל־יְקֹוָק
וּבָכֹה תִבְכֶּה: (יא) וַתִּדֹּר נֶדֶר וַתֹּאמַר יְקֹוָק צְבָאוֹת אִם־רָאֹה תִרְאֶה בָּעֳנִי
אֲמָתֶךָ וּזְכַרְתַּנִי וְלֹא־תִשְׁכַּח אֶת־אֲמָתֶךָ וְנָתַתָּה לַאֲמָתְךָ זֶרַע אֲנָשִׁים וּנְתַתִּיו
לַיקֹוָק כָּל־יְמֵי חַיָּיו וּמוֹרָה לֹא־יַעֲלֶה עַל־רֹאשׁוֹ:

Chana arose after eating at Shilo and after drinking — now Eli the priest was sitting on a throne by the doorpost of the great hall of the Lord. And she was bitter of feelings so she prayed to the Lord while she wept, yes, wept. She vowed a vow: "O Lord of Hosts, if You will see, yes see, the affliction of Your maidservant and will bear me in mind and not forget Your maidservant, and will give Your maidservant seed of men, I will dedicate him to the Lord for all the days of his life; and no razor shall go up on his head" (I Shemuel 1:9-11).

There is no record of what she said. The only perceptible expressions are tears and weeping. Then, out of the bitterness that has brought her to prayer, she takes her stand. She makes a vow. This is risky. Making a vow whose central component is a bargain creates an equilibrium between herself, a finite human, and God, who is infinite. She says to God, "If you give me a child, I will give the child back to You." She is dealing with God as if with an equal. Only someone like Chana, possessed of a consistent depth of relationship with the one God, can take such a stance. Only someone such as

Chana, who has emptied herself of everything but tears, has the standing to talk with God this way. Only someone as humble as Chana can be as brazen as Chana.

Following the vow, she increases her prayer. Thus, the vow and the bargain are enveloped by prayer itself. The prayer that follows the bargain is once again silent. In this state of intimacy with God, Eli imagines her a drunk and insults her. He confronts her, "Give up the wine!" Chana responds patiently, as if instructing a child. She teaches him that not all who appear to be drunk have had wine.

In response to Eli's accusation, Chana first teaches him about the ways of prayer. He approached her in ignorance of the ways of talking with God in silence. Only after teaching him about prayer does she directly address his accusation, which is grave and ironic. She continues to instruct the high priest. Take note of her words as she confronts Eli with the import of his accusation. If she is drunk, then indeed she is a person rightly characterized as *beliyya'al*, "base."

שמואל א פרק א (טז) אַל־תִּתֵּן אֶת־אֲמָתְךָ לִפְנֵי בַּת־בְּלִיָּעַל ...

Do not consider your maidservant a base woman ... (I Shemuel 1:16).

She will not let Eli avoid the implications of accusing her of drunkenness in the Mishkan. This word — *beliyya'al* — is employed in TaNaKh to describe corrupting idolators. It characterizes the murderers of Yavesh Gilead. *Beliyya'al* encompasses far more than baseness. In biblical usage, such a person is cruel and corrupt, lacking a moral calculus. Why, then, does Chana employ such a term? Does she hear this indictment in Eli's words? Drunkenness in the Sanctuary is indeed *beliyya'al*. In most cases, *beliyya'al* refers to those who must appear in trial before a divine or human court. *Beliyya'al* fits Chana's purpose, expressed in prayer as intercession for a judgment from the divine judge. She pleas before God not to judge her as one of those base figures who will receive an unfavorable response from the court.

And in an exquisite irony, her son, Shemuel, will ultimately bring Eli notice that his sons are truly *beliyya'al.* Her son will come to know God, whom Eli's sons do not know.

שמואל א פרק ב (יב) וּבְנֵי עֵלִי בְּנֵי בְלִיָּעַל לֹא יָדְעוּ אֶת־יְקֹוָק:

Now Eli's sons were base men; they knew not the Lord (I Shemuel 2:12).

10

Eli's Response

Chana's response to Eli's accusation of intoxication is instructive. It is credible because she is authentic. Eli withdraws his accusation and blesses her.

שמואל א פרק א (יז) וַיַּעַן עֵלִי וַיֹּאמֶר לְכִי לְשָׁלוֹם וֵאלֹהֵי יִשְׂרָאֵל יִתֵּן אֶת־שֵׁלָתֵךְ אֲשֶׁר שָׁאַלְתְּ מֵעִמּוֹ:

"Then go in peace," said Eli, "and may the God of Israel grant the request you have asked of Him" (I Shemuel 1:17).

Eli gives her the *berakhah* of *shalom*, and then goes a step further: He confirms the legitimacy of the bargain she has made with God. Eli the High Priest recognizes the truth of Chana's reply to him. Listening to her response, he realizes that he is in the presence of a great spiritual personality. Now he knows she is not drunk. Eli has been taught the ways of the service of the heart. He has learned her *tefila*.

We then read:

שמואל א פרק א (יח) וַתֹּאמֶר תִּמְצָא שִׁפְחָתְךָ חֵן בְּעֵינֶיךָ וַתֵּלֶךְ הָאִשָּׁה לְדַרְכָּהּ וַתֹּאכַל וּפָנֶיהָ לֹא־הָיוּ־לָהּ עוֹד:

She answered, "May your handmaid find favor in your eyes"; and the woman went on her way, and she ate, and her face was no longer [sad] on her" (I Shemuel 1:18).

Though she has not yet received a response to her proposed bargain with God, Chana has gained acknowledgment from the high priest that she is a person of integrity, and that her *tefila* is presented in sincerity and authenticity. With Eli's blessing, Chana affirms that someone has heard her prayer and recognized her plight.

Eli's understanding engenders integral changes in Chana. She knows she is not alone, for she has found favor in Eli's eyes. No one looks upon the abandoned, but she is now secure in the unique path she will follow. She, who in bitterness could not eat, can now feed herself.

These changes culminate in a new face presented to the world. She is a different person, transformed in the knowledge that she is not alone and not forgotten. She has been heard. The only woman to enter the Mishkan came into the presence without husband, friend, or community. In crossing the threshold guarded by Eli, she pursues a singular path. In her abandonment, she is taken for a drunkard. No more. She acquires a new face, a new presence. Chana prays in a state of abandonment; Eli meets her in that place of solitude where she is transformed. Her reunion with Elkana and Peninna is not recorded. We can only imagine how they receive this new Chana.

At this point, we must pause to ensure we have not too quickly dismissed the import of seemingly prosaic words. The Hebrew language of TaNaKh is dense and abrupt. So much can be conveyed with just one verb.

Chana was able to enter the Mishkan and to pray only after she took the counsel of her beloved husband and ate. She had been fasting, possibly in despair or mourning, or possibly in preparation for prayer. We cannot ignore that, immediately following her prayerful experience, she eats once again. Her entry into the Mishkan is preceded by eating and her exit is followed by eating. Her prayerful experience is bracketed by eating.

When Chana eats prior to entry into the Mishkan, it must be understood in relation to the previous verse, in which not eating was a sign of distress and lamentation akin to a fast day. After Elkana's counsel, she eats, but remains deeply embittered. Following her encounter with God and Eli, she eats for the second time. This meal is the inverse of the earlier situation. Chana's ability to eat, perhaps even to feast, may be a celebration: Inherent in the response of the high priest is the hint of divine understanding. At the very least, it is a sign that the despair that nurtured her has slipped away. (I am grateful to Jon Levenson for this idea.)

11

From Tabernacle to Home and Birth

Like Sarah, Rebecca, Rachel, and Leah — the other purposefully barren women — Chana is remembered by God.

שמואל א פרק א (יט) וַיַּשְׁכִּמוּ בַבֹּקֶר וַיִּשְׁתַּחֲווּ לִפְנֵי יְקֹוָק וַיָּשֻׁבוּ וַיָּבֹאוּ אֶל־בֵּיתָם הָרָמָתָה וַיֵּדַע אֶלְקָנָה אֶת־חַנָּה אִשְׁתּוֹ וַיִּזְכְּרֶהָ יְקֹוָק׃

Early next morning they bowed low before the Lord, and they went back home to Ramah. Elkana knew his wife Chana and the Lord remembered her (I Shemuel 1:19).

This is instructive. After Peninna's torment and Eli's accusation, Chana serves God once more, her prayerful posture remaining untroubled. Before returning home, she "bows low before the Lord." Her *tefila* is once again inaudible and unknown.

Chana and Elkana return home to Ramah. Elkana, who accepted her barrenness, now knows his wife anew as her God remembers her. Similarly, after they learn they are mortal, Adam knows Chava so that all life may continue. Those whose future holds the key to continuity conceive and birth with the verb "to know." Without Shemuel, Israel's national history cannot emerge from the chaos of the era of the Judges into the epoch that will give Israel David, the monarch who will unite the Twelve Tribes. Just as Adam knew Chava, Elkana knew his wife. Chava is known after banishment from the Garden. Chana is known after entry into the Garden's successor, the Mishkan. When Elkana knew Chana, God remembered her.

Her prayers are answered. When she gives birth to a son, she declares his name Shemuel.

שמואל א פרק א (כ) וַיְהִי לִתְקֻפוֹת הַיָּמִים וַתַּהַר חַנָּה וַתֵּלֶד בֵּן וַתִּקְרָא אֶת־שְׁמוֹ שְׁמוּאֵל כִּי מֵיְקֹוָק שְׁאִלְתִּיו:

Chana conceived, and at the turn of the year bore a son. She named him Shemuel, meaning, "I asked the Lord for him" (I Shemuel 1:20).

She keeps the child at home. A regular at the Mishkan of Shilo, she will now absent herself for several years. Shemuel cannot come to the Mishkan as a baby or a toddler. At the same time, Chana understands that service to God will not wait until adulthood. He is dedicated to God. As soon as he can eat and move about on his own, his spiritual formation will begin. He is God's from the womb.

שמואל א פרק א (כב) וְחַנָּה לֹא עָלָתָה כִּי־אָמְרָה לְאִישָׁהּ עַד יִגָּמֵל הַנַּעַר וַהֲבִאֹתִיו וְנִרְאָה אֶת־פְּנֵי יְקֹוָק וְיָשַׁב שָׁם עַד־עוֹלָם:

Chana did not go up (to the Mishkan). She said to her husband, "When the child is weaned, I will bring him. For when he beholds the presence of the Lord, he must remain there for good" (I Shemuel 1:22).

Chana does not bring the baby Shemuel up to the Mishkan until he has been weaned. There is nourishment that one gets only in mother's milk, especially when that mother is the exceptional *mitpalelet* of TaNaKh. She plays a critical a role in his spiritual formation. When he is brought to Eli the High Priest, he will mature in the Mishkan bathed in the light of God's presence. Given that Chana is a *mitpalelet*, the songs, the baby talk, and the language instruction that will envelop Shemuel will be the stuff of *tefila*. It will be the language of relationship with God. Given Chana's intimacy with the Kadosh Barukh Hu, the maternal love of a believer and the love of God will nurture him until he is weaned and brought up to the Mishkan. Her prayer gets a child of God; her *tefila* cultivates the personality of that child.

In keeping her promise to God, Chana adds an uncommon phrase. It is only Jacob and Moshe who behold the presence. She is now confident that when she brings the young Shemuel up to the Mishkan, he too will behold the presence. Thus, we gain the meaning of a verse in Tehilim.

תהלים פרק צט (ו) מֹשֶׁה וְאַהֲרֹן בְּכֹהֲנָיו וּשְׁמוּאֵל בְּקֹרְאֵי שְׁמוֹ ...

Moshe and Aharon were among His priests, as was Shemuel, they were the ones who called upon Him by name (Tehilim 99:6).

The *mitpalelet* par excellence prayed a child into being who, like Moshe and Aharon, knew and called upon the name. It is now to the place of the name that Chana returns. When and how will she fulfill her vow to return the child to the service of the Lord?

12

The Return to Shiloh: Promise Kept

What will Chana do on the return to Shilo? The barren one of Ramah now returns to Shiloh as a mother — but she is no ordinary mother. She is the only woman to have entered the Sanctuary, the only barren one to contract a child of God. Chana fulfills her agreement. When Shemuel is weaned she brings him to the service of God, to Eli the High Priest, in the Mishkan at Shiloh. He who thought her drunk now receives the child born of her prayer. She does this to the accompaniment of thanksgiving offerings aplenty.

שמואל א פרק א (כד) וַתַּעֲלֵהוּ עִמָּהּ כַּאֲשֶׁר גְּמָלַתּוּ בְּפָרִים שְׁלֹשָׁה וְאֵיפָה
אַחַת קֶמַח וְנֵבֶל יַיִן וַתְּבִאֵהוּ בֵית־יְקֹוָק שִׁלוֹ וְהַנַּעַר נָעַר: (כה) וַיִּשְׁחֲטוּ אֶת־
הַפָּר וַיָּבִיאוּ אֶת־הַנַּעַר אֶל־עֵלִי:

When she had weaned him, she took him up with her, along with three bulls, one ephah of flour, and a jar of wine. And though the boy was still very young, she brought him to the House of the Lord at Shiloh. After slaughtering the bull, they brought the boy to Eli (I Shemuel 1:24, 25).

She meets Eli. Presenting the boy to him, she must once again instruct him.

שמואל א פרק א (כו) וַתֹּאמֶר בִּי אֲדֹנִי חֵי נַפְשְׁךָ אֲדֹנִי אֲנִי הָאִשָּׁה הַנִּצֶּבֶת
עִמְּכָה בָּזֶה לְהִתְפַּלֵּל אֶל־יְקֹוָק: (כז) אֶל־הַנַּעַר הַזֶּה הִתְפַּלָּלְתִּי וַיִּתֵּן יְקֹוָק לִי
אֶת־שְׁאֵלָתִי אֲשֶׁר שָׁאַלְתִּי מֵעִמּוֹ: (כח) וְגַם אָנֹכִי הִשְׁאִלְתִּהוּ לַיקֹוָק כָּל־הַיָּמִים
אֲשֶׁר הָיָה הוּא שָׁאוּל לַיקֹוָק וַיִּשְׁתַּחוּ שָׁם לַיקֹוָק:

She said, "Please, my lord! As you live, my lord, I am the woman who stood here with you and prayed to the Lord. It was this boy I prayed for; and the

> Lord has granted me what I asked of Him. I, in turn, lend him on request to the Lord. For as long as he lives he is lent on request to the Lord." And they bowed low there before the Lord (I Shemuel 1:26-28).

Twice now Eli does not recognize her. Twice she is invisible to him. The first time, he takes her for a drunk; he does not look at her face and recognize a woman praying to God out of the depths of torment. The second time, Eli does not recognize her as a mother, filled with the radiance of God's gift to her.

Chana presents herself to Eli. Listen to her every word: "Please, my master, by your very life ..." Note she says *please.* She seeks the favor of recognition. She speaks in the language of an oath — "by your very life." *By your very life I affirm who I am. You know me. I am the one woman who entered the Mishkan. I am the one you took for a drunkard. I am the one who entered the Sanctuary with bitter life and hardened personality. I am the one you blessed. The blessing has come to be. I am here with the child I sought from God. I am the one with whom you stood in prayer. I am the only woman to stand in prayer in the Mishkan. I stood there with you. I taught you the ways of silent, intimate prayer of the heart. You should recognize me. I stood with you when I dared to intercede with God in order to get a child. That is who I am. You gave me your blessing.* All this is captured in her eight Hebrew words: "I am the woman who stood here with you and prayed to the Lord."

In this declaration, Chana reveals something new about the experience of standing in *tefila* in the Mishkan, something the narrator did not tell us at the time. This is a retrospective declaration to Eli the High Priest, who does not recognize her. She now reveals a secret: When she stood in *tefila* in the Mishkan, we did not know the location of Eli the High Priest. As she began to pray, where was he? Was he sitting in his chair? Did he stand up and turn around to look at her? Did he move closer to observe her, to attempt to hear what she was presenting to God?

We are told none of this. Several years later, on her return to Shilo, as she reintroduces herself to Eli, she tells us something about her experience of *tefila* that we as yet do not know. She identifies herself, "I am the woman who stood here beside you and prayed to the Lord. You have stood with no other woman in prayer." Or, more precisely, "I stood with you in prayer. You were standing alongside me. You came so near that you were with me as I prayed. I am the only woman next to whom you stood as she prayed. You stood with me in my prayer."

Chana is the only woman to have entered the Sanctuary, and now we know she is the only woman with whom the high priest stood in prayer. She reminds Eli that he heard her pray for a child. She is the *nitzevet*, the woman who stood in prayer with the high priest. She informs him that his blessing has been fulfilled. She declares that she has come to fulfill her vow. With these words, "I am the woman who stood with you in prayer ...," she presents the child Shemuel to Eli.

Why does Eli not recognize her? She is transformed, not just by the birth of the baby. She is a woman now formed by having nursed Shemuel for several years. She left Shiloh barren and blessed; she returns as a mother. Eli does not know this Chana. He meets her again for the first time. Having presented herself, she introduces the boy. "This is the child for whom I interceded, prayed, judged, and contracted." Shemuel is the work of Chana's prayer. He is the one for whom Chana dared contract with the Almighty. "For this child did I pray; I prayed this child from the very hand of God. This is not a normal child. This is not a child regularly conceived and birthed. This is a child born of my intercession and my contract prayer."

It is not just that she presents Shemuel to Eli when she declares, "It was for this boy that I prayed." As we have noted, the Hebrew for "I prayed" is the intensive reflexive *hitpalalti*, "I have used my very self to intercede." *It was for this boy that I interceded with God. It was for this boy that I brought my judgment before God. He is fruit of my prayerful service. I prayed him into life. Shemuel, in his very being, is the child of a prayer.*

The child God gave Chana, she now returns to God in fulfillment of her vow. In Shemuel's name, Chana memorializes her contract with God. The name Shemuel puns with *sha'al*, "asked" or "borrowed" of God. Chana now declares that he is *sha'ul* — "returned" in loan to God. In his name is inscribed for all to witness that he was sought from God and returned to God. God and Chana have fulfilled their obligations to each other.

At this point, Chana's selflessness and devotion to God again invite comparison with the first barren woman, Sarah, and by extension, Avraham as well. In both instances the child, long sought of God, must be returned to God. Chana, however, does so of her own initiative, out of the depths of her understanding of her son's assignment and her role in fulfilling God's will. That is not the case with Avraham and Sarah. Isaac, the child long sought in their barrenness, must be given to God. However, Avraham and Sarah do not come to that on their own, as does Chana. God has to instruct Avraham to bring Isaac as an offering to Moriah.

Here a digression is needed to avoid any misunderstanding. Nothing happened to Isaac. He was bound on the altar. That was it. The knife did not touch his throat. The fire was not kindled. He was not consumed by the unkindled fire, nor was he reduced to ashes, nor were those ashes heaped before the glory throne, nor was he resurrected by the life-giving dew. *Ein miqra yotse mi-ydei peshuto* — "scripture never departs from its plain meaning." Nothing happened to Isaac. He came to Moriah alive and well, and left much the same way. That is why the next passage in the Torah announces the birth of Rebecca, his soon-to-be wife.

The Akedah is the fitting conclusion to the educational odyssey of Avraham and Sarah. Their life story begins with a notice that sets the agenda for their development: "... and

Sarah was barren, she had no child." One of the central life lessons that Avraham and Sarah must learn is the meaning of barrenness and birth. In barrenness lies the promise of birth. They must learn that the Kadosh Barukh Hu, who created all life in six days, continues to be the master of life and creation. These two, Avraham and Sarah, believe there is none but the one God, the Creator — who is denied His creatorship beyond the six days of creation.

They are promised that the land will be given to their children, and that their children will become a great nation. Promise follows promise, yet they have no children. They doubt the word of God. They offer alternatives: The manager of their estate, Eliezer of Damascus, can be the successor. Ishmael can be the successor. When told that the successor, the next patriarch, will be the child of Avraham and Sarah, they both mock God.

בראשית פרשת לך לך פרק יז (יז) וַיִּפֹּל אַבְרָהָם עַל־פָּנָיו וַיִּצְחָק וַיֹּאמֶר בְּלִבּוֹ הַלְּבֶן מֵאָה־שָׁנָה יִוָּלֵד וְאִם־שָׂרָה הֲבַת־תִּשְׁעִים שָׁנָה תֵּלֵד: (יח) וַיֹּאמֶר אַבְרָהָם אֶל־הָאֱלֹהִים לוּ יִשְׁמָעֵאל יִחְיֶה לְפָנֶיךָ:

Avraham threw himself on his face and laughed, as he said to himself, "Can a child be born to a man 100 years old, or can Sarah bear a child at 90?" And Avraham said to God, "O that Ishmael might live by Your favor!" (Be-Reshit 17:17, 18).

בראשית פרשת וירא פרק יח (יב) וַתִּצְחַק שָׂרָה בְּקִרְבָּהּ לֵאמֹר אַחֲרֵי בְלֹתִי הָיְתָה־לִּי עֶדְנָה וַאדֹנִי זָקֵן:

And Sarah laughed to herself, saying, "Now that I am withered, am I to have Eden-like flow — with my husband so old?" (Be-Reshit 18:12).

Following this unresolved confrontation with God, a few chapters later another issue of fertility emerges. King Avimelekh has taken Sarah to his palace not realizing that she is the wife of Avraham. God afflicted the estate of Avimelekh with sterility for taking Sarah. Yet, there is to be remission of this punishment because Avimelekh did not know that Sarah is the wife of Avraham. God instructs Avimelekh to ask Avraham to intercede on his behalf with Him. Avraham intercedes with God. Fertility is restored to Avimelekh's household. Following that, Sarah becomes pregnant.

בראשית פרשת וירא פרק כ (יז) וַיִּתְפַּלֵּל אַבְרָהָם אֶל־הָאֱלֹהִים וַיִּרְפָּא אֱלֹהִים אֶת־אֲבִימֶלֶךְ וְאֶת־אִשְׁתּוֹ וְאַמְהֹתָיו וַיֵּלֵדוּ: (יח) כִּי־עָצֹר עָצַר יְקוָק בְּעַד כָּל־רֶחֶם לְבֵית אֲבִימֶלֶךְ עַל־דְּבַר שָׂרָה אֵשֶׁת אַבְרָהָם:

Avraham then interceded with God, and God healed Avimelekh and his wife and his slave girls, so that they bore children; for the Lord had closed fast every womb of the household of Avimelekh because of Sarah, the wife of Avraham (Be-Reshit 20:17, 18).

בראשית פרשת וירא פרק כא (א) וַיקוָק פָּקַד אֶת־שָׂרָה כַּאֲשֶׁר אָמָר וַיַּעַשׂ יְקוָק לְשָׂרָה כַּאֲשֶׁר דִּבֵּר: (ב) וַתַּהַר וַתֵּלֶד שָׂרָה לְאַבְרָהָם בֵּן לִזְקֻנָיו לַמּוֹעֵד אֲשֶׁר־דִּבֶּר אֹתוֹ אֱלֹהִים:

The Lord took note of Sarah as He had promised, and the Lord did for Sarah as He had spoken. Sarah conceived and bore a son to Avraham in his old age, at the set time of which God had spoken (Be-Reshit 21:1, 2).

From the Avimelekh episode, Avraham and Sarah learn that the creation of life is in God's hands long after the six creation days. Now they are summoned to the test of the Akedah. God in effect is saying to Avraham: *You two, alone in the whole world, know that I am the one God who has created Heaven and earth. Yet when I told you that you would have a child, you laughed at me. Well now comes the test. If you really, really believe that in your withered old age I created life with the two of you; if you really, really believe that I am the one who gave you Isaac, then you will give Isaac back to me.*

This makes perfect sense, for if you really believe that, in your withered old age, God has miraculously given you a child, you'd surely give the child to God. The test of the Akedah is to give the child back to God. The promise of the Akedah is that, if you do so, the child will be returned to you. Avraham passed the test. Isaac is returned.

The Akedah is the culmination of a saga whose purpose was disclosed at the very outset of the saga of Avraham and Sarah. Sarah was barren. How will she birth? God continues to be master of life long after the six days of creation. In the end, Avraham and Sarah learned the lesson well. Nothing happened to Isaac. Chana prayed a child from God because, from the outset, she knew her barrenness had purpose, and so she returns the child to God. It is this belief that inspires her song.

13

Thanksgiving Song

We are now at a critical juncture. More service of the heart, *avoda shebalev,* awaits a woman of Chana's spiritual stature. The prayer of the barren Chana has been answered. She has conceived and birthed a son, and fulfilled her obligation to dedicate the son that God has given her to the service of God. She is a person of prayer integrity. The woman who began in hardened spirit, bitter unto life in God's presence, now presents her transformed self. Chana gives thanksgiving to God. Her epic poem endures as the climax of the Haftara for the first day of Rosh HaShana.

Chana returns to the presence of God, to the Mishkan, which she entered years earlier. God and Chana are now bound together. They conceived this child. She who began in bitterness now sings to God.

As noted earlier, Chana comes onto the stage of Jewish history at a time of chaos following a set of deeply disturbing events. This literary pattern is found elsewhere in TaNaKh. After the announcement of national enslavement in Egypt, the Torah presents the story of one family whose child, Moshe, will grow and develop into the national leader. Moshe will also be brought to the stage of history by not one, but several women. The events described in the closing chapters of the Book of Judges, known as the Concubine of Giva, set the stage for the drama of Chana. These events present barrenness on a national scale: the murder of one person, the slaughter and near extinction of the Tribe of Benjamin, the killing of the men of Yavesh Gilead, and the unimaginable mating drama at Shilo to reverse the decline in the Tribe of Benjamin. The extreme steps taken to ensure the survival of Benjamin represent death and desolation in the service of fertility.

Chana realizes that national barrenness is embodied in her very person. As a counterpoint to what she has just witnessed, she turns her heart to God in testimony that the God of history is moved through the intercession of *tefila*. She travels from the national and communal to the personal, and from the personal to the national and communal. She looks backward at the horrific events. These summon her to *tefila*, to petition and contract. In so doing, she is able to look forward to the birth of a son dedicated to God and the restoration of Israel. She does the work of *tefila* at a moment of national chaos and personal tragedy. She now reads her personal drama into the national epic of Israel.

As we approach the epic thanksgiving song and prayer of Chana, let us retrace the prayer terrain she has walked to arrive at this moment. We met her first when she, along with her family, brought *korbanot,* animal and cereal offerings, to the Mishkan. This is the regular devotion of the family of Elkana. She moves from *korban* to first *tefila*, tears, bitterness, silence, and bargain. The brazen proposal of a contract with God is possible, for she has achieved intimacy with God. Following the vow, once again she engages in *tefila*, and is challenged by Eli. Chana prostrates herself before taking leave of Shilo and the presence of God to return home, secure in Eli's blessing that God will accept her contract and offer. Having birthed the child and kept her promise to return him to the service of God, Chana once again brings *korban*, thanksgiving offering, in celebration to God at Shilo. This is the point of the story at which we find ourselves. The culmination of her prayerful career once again begins in *korban* and moves to *tefila*, the presentation of her thanksgiving song.

The message in this pattern should not be lost. *Korban* is a necessary, yet insufficient condition for intimacy with the one God. On both occasions, after she brings an offering, she turns to God in the depth of conversation expressed in prayerful intercession. After the offering of *korban*, she offers prayer. *Korban* opens the gate to *tefila*.

In this prayerful saga, the text records six distinct experiences in which Chana worships and prays to the Kadosh Barukh Hu. Initially, she eats and drinks and enters the Mishkan.

שמואל א פרק א (י) וְהִיא מָרַת נָפֶשׁ וַתִּתְפַּלֵּל עַל־יְקֹוָק וּבָכֹה תִבְכֶּה:

In her wretchedness, she prayed to the Lord, weeping all the while (I Shemuel 1:10).

Next, she makes a bargain with God, secured by an oath.

שמואל א פרק א (יא) וַתִּדֹּר נֶדֶר וַתֹּאמַר יְקֹוָק צְבָאוֹת אִם־רָאֹה תִרְאֶה בָּעֳנִי אֲמָתֶךָ וּזְכַרְתַּנִי וְלֹא־תִשְׁכַּח אֶת־אֲמָתֶךָ וְנָתַתָּה לַאֲמָתְךָ זֶרַע אֲנָשִׁים וּנְתַתִּיו לַיקֹוָק כָּל־יְמֵי חַיָּיו וּמוֹרָה לֹא־יַעֲלֶה עַל־רֹאשׁוֹ:

And she made this vow: "O Lord of Hosts, if You will look upon the suffering of Your maidservant and will remember me and not forget Your maidservant, and if You will grant Your maidservant a male child, I will dedicate him to the Lord for all the days of his life; and no razor shall ever touch his head" (I Shemuel 1:11).

After concluding the contract, she turns again to classic *tefila*, praying to God for a child.

שמואל א פרק א (יב) וְהָיָה כִּי הִרְבְּתָה לְהִתְפַּלֵּל לִפְנֵי יְקֹוָק וְעֵלִי שֹׁמֵר אֶת־פִּיהָ:

As she kept on praying before the Lord, Eli watched her mouth (I Shemuel 1:12).

After Eli the High Priest gives her the blessing that her prayer request will be answered, she worships once again before returning home to Shilo.

שמואל א פרק א (יט) וַיַּשְׁכִּמוּ בַבֹּקֶר וַיִּשְׁתַּחֲווּ לִפְנֵי יְקֹוָק וַיָּשֻׁבוּ וַיָּבֹאוּ אֶל־
בֵּיתָם הָרָמָתָה וַיֵּדַע אֶלְקָנָה אֶת־חַנָּה אִשְׁתּוֹ וַיִּזְכְּרֶהָ יְקֹוָק:

Early next morning they bowed low before the Lord, and they went back home to Ramah. Elkana knew his wife Chana and the Lord remembered her (I Shemuel 1:19).

She births Shemuel and keeps him at home until he is weaned. In fulfillment of her promise, she returns the child to God at Shilo. When she arrives, she worships God.

שמואל א פרק א (כד) וַתַּעֲלֵהוּ עִמָּהּ כַּאֲשֶׁר גְּמָלַתּוּ בְּפָרִים שְׁלֹשָׁה וְאֵיפָה
אַחַת קֶמַח וְנֵבֶל יַיִן וַתְּבִאֵהוּ בֵית־יְקֹוָק שִׁלוֹ וְהַנַּעַר נָעַר: (כה) וַיִּשְׁחֲטוּ אֶת־
הַפָּר וַיָּבִיאוּ אֶת־הַנַּעַר אֶל־עֵלִי:

When she had weaned him, she took him up with her, along with three bulls, one ephah of flour, and a jar of wine. And though the boy was still very young, she brought him to the House of the Lord at Shiloh. After slaughtering the bull, they brought the boy to Eli (I Shemuel 1:24, 25).

In the prayerful life of Chana, described in but a few verses, we watch her at prayer and worship six times. Following the fulfillment of her promise to dedicate the child to God, accompanied by offering, Chana presents her song of thanksgiving to God.

Shirat Chana — The Thanksgiving Song of Chana

שמואל א פרק ב
(א) וַתִּתְפַּלֵּל חַנָּה וַתֹּאמַר עָלַץ לִבִּי בַּיקֹוָק רָמָה קַרְנִי בַּיקֹוָק רָחַב פִּי עַל־
אוֹיְבַי כִּי שָׂמַחְתִּי בִּישׁוּעָתֶךָ:

(ב) אֵין־קָדוֹשׁ כַּיקֹוָק כִּי אֵין בִּלְתֶּךָ וְאֵין צוּר כֵּאלֹהֵינוּ:
(ג) אַל־תַּרְבּוּ תְדַבְּרוּ גְּבֹהָה גְבֹהָה יֵצֵא עָתָק מִפִּיכֶם כִּי אֵל דֵּעוֹת יְקֹוָק ולא וְלוֹ נִתְכְּנוּ עֲלִלוֹת:
(ד) קֶשֶׁת גִּבֹּרִים חַתִּים וְנִכְשָׁלִים אָזְרוּ חָיִל:
(ה) שְׂבֵעִים בַּלֶּחֶם נִשְׂכָּרוּ וּרְעֵבִים חָדֵלּוּ עַד־עֲקָרָה יָלְדָה שִׁבְעָה וְרַבַּת בָּנִים אֻמְלָלָה:
(ו) יְקֹוָק מֵמִית וּמְחַיֶּה מוֹרִיד שְׁאוֹל וַיָּעַל:
(ז) יְקֹוָק מוֹרִישׁ וּמַעֲשִׁיר מַשְׁפִּיל אַף־מְרוֹמֵם:
(ח) מֵקִים מֵעָפָר דָּל מֵאַשְׁפֹּת יָרִים אֶבְיוֹן לְהוֹשִׁיב עִם־נְדִיבִים וְכִסֵּא כָבוֹד יַנְחִלֵם כִּי לַיקֹוָק מְצֻקֵי אֶרֶץ וַיָּשֶׁת עֲלֵיהֶם תֵּבֵל:
(ט) רַגְלֵי חסידו חֲסִידָיו יִשְׁמֹר וּרְשָׁעִים בַּחֹשֶׁךְ יִדָּמּוּ כִּי־לֹא בְכֹחַ יִגְבַּר־אִישׁ:
(י) יְקֹוָק יֵחַתּוּ מריבו מְרִיבָיו עלו עָלָיו בַּשָּׁמַיִם יַרְעֵם יְקֹוָק יָדִין אַפְסֵי־אָרֶץ וְיִתֶּן־עֹז לְמַלְכּוֹ וְיָרֵם קֶרֶן מְשִׁיחוֹ

Section 1: Introduction and Statement of Purpose

1. And Chana prayed: My heart exults in the Lord;
My horn is exalted through the Lord.
I gloat over my enemies;
I rejoice in Your deliverance.
2. There is no holy one like the Lord,
Truly, there is none beside You;
There is no rock like our God.
3. Talk no more with lofty pride,
Let no arrogance cross your lips!
For the Lord is an all-knowing God;
By Him actions [human events, history] are measured.

Section 2: Thanksgiving to God, Master of Inversions

4. The bows of the mighty are broken,
And the faltering are girded with strength.
5. Men once sated must hire out for bread;

Men once hungry hunger no more.
While the barren woman bears seven,
The mother of many is forlorn.
6. The Lord deals death and gives life,
Casts down into Sheol and raises up.
7. The Lord makes poor and makes rich;
He casts down,
He also lifts high.
8. He raises the poor from the dust,
Lifts up the needy from the dunghill,
Setting them with nobles,
Granting them seats of honor.
For the pillars of the earth are the Lord's;
He has set the world upon them.

Section 3: Prophecy and Crescendo

9. He guards the steps of His faithful,
But the wicked perish in darkness —
For not by strength shall man prevail.
10. The foes of the Lord shall be shattered;
He will thunder against them in the Heavens.
The Lord will judge the ends of the earth.
He will give power to His king,
And exalt the horn of His anointed one
(I Shemuel 2:1-10).

The Song of Chana is ten verses long. The first three verses are introductory. The key ideas of this spiritual epic poem are expressed in the main body, verses four through eight. Verses nine and ten are the culmination of the song in prophecy. There is continuity in Chana's opening words, as she alludes to the path she has walked in her heart with God. She who was suffering in her heart came to God by talking to Him in her heart. She now prays and exults with her heart.

In the introductory verses, Chana tells us who she is and why she offers this song and prayer — "My heart rejoices in God." This is the same person who once spoke in her heart with hardened bitterness and tears. She sings this song because she is now filled with the joy of God's goodness. After she alludes to her experience that births the song, she describes why God should be praised and thanked. Indeed, one of the features of thanksgiving psalms is the focus on God's deeds, rather than the experience of the one who benefits from His gifts. God is incomparably Kadosh — utterly distinct and unique. There is no strength in the world like God's.

She warns that human beings, especially those who are intellectually corrupt, should talk less. They should not boast about their understanding of human affairs. The course of history is determined by God. God is a God of wisdom. In recognition of God's knowledge and providential direction of human affairs, man and woman should stand in awe and humility. Only those as humble as Chana or Moshe can be brazen with God. Having established God's intentional guidance of the life course of the individual, Chana moves to the substance of the song itself.

Once again, her personal situation inspires her to great ideas of belief. She looks beyond her self to the human condition, the waves of change and alternating realities of life. Humans experience wealth and poverty, power and weakness, hunger and plenty, glory and defeat, health and sickness, life and death. This she knows from her experience of moving from barrenness to fertility.

These are some of the varieties of human experience expressing the regular defeats and triumphs of the human condition. The central idea of Chana's thanksgiving poem is that these opposing experiences of life are not accidental. Human affairs are in the hands of the God of history who intervenes in individual lives. Too often arrogant persons assert they know the mysteries of life. They do not understand the role that God plays in each and every life circumstance. Indeed, no one condition can ever be trusted for permanence. The bow of the warrior is broken and the faltering weak are girded with strength. Those well fed now hire out for food. Those hungry are nourished. In the middle of the song she presents another contrast. She thanks God that she who was barren birthed "seven" (a figurative or symbolic number representing wholesomeness) and the "one of many children" who mocked her is now forsaken. She continues with juxtapositions to describe God's interventions in human affairs. God brings life and death. He casts down into Sheol and raises up. He brings riches and poverty. He raises up the poor from the dust and the destitute from the dung heap, seating them with the mighty and the honorable.

There are some who fear that Chana's song opens with triumphalism and possibly vengeance, when she declares, "I have triumphed over my enemies!" Modern enlightened sensibilities rarely permit the term *enemy*. It is reserved for those who have committed apostasy to evil. *Enemy* is simply not used for those with whom one disagrees, or to describe those who have caused pain and aggravation in the normal course of familial, social, and communal affairs. It is a term reserved for deeply hostile and evil persons or nations seeking to cause great irreparable harm, and with whom there is no possibility of reconciliation. In TaNaKh, the word *enemy* is not restricted to such persons or parties. Amalek, who seeks to destroy Israel, is an enemy that fits contemporary sensibilities. Amalek is a genocidal monster.

Short of such distinction, many are capable of evil thoughts and evil designs, and even a few evil actions. However, the term *enemy* in TaNaKh also refers to those who present ideologies or plans contrary to God's Torah and intentions. Chana, for example, has a trust in God not shared by Peninna, not even by her Elkana, and not by Eli. Peninna is not a bad person; she is an average person. She is in competition with Chana for primacy in the family of Elkana. Peninna sees

Chana's barrenness not just as necessary for her own status. It is worse than that: Peninna sees Chana's barrenness as a human condition. She does not see it as related to God in any way.

Elkana, who surely loves Chana, sees her barrenness in much the same way. It is a human phenomenon. Elkana could have prayed, or better yet interceded with God on behalf of his wife, as Isaac did long ago for Rebecca. He does not. He is unable to believe that God has closed Chana's womb.

Chana's act of petition to and bargain with God is a rebuke to both of them. She sees God's hand at work in her personal experience of barrenness. Elkana and Peninna are believers in God. They see God's hand at work in the national history of ancient Israel. However, they do not see God's hand at work in the life of Chana, or any one individual. They oppose Chana's belief that God's attentive diligence to the human condition is expressed in her barrenness, and that only in the encounter with God will she gain a child. They are both enemies of the exalted and thoughtful understandings of Chana.

Eli is also an ideological enemy. He knows that Chana is barren. He has witnessed her childlessness throughout the years of her pilgrimages to Shiloh. When Eli saw Chana standing in rapt attention, her lips moving, silence emerging, he should have immediately connected that to her barrenness. He did not. He, too, did not identify with Chana's belief that her personal circumstance is an expression of divine will.

Chana believed all along that God had closed her womb, and that only in the encounter with God would the door of her womb be opened. Chana's belief triumphs over her enemies.

For Chana, God's omnipotence is manifest in the power to determine who to life, who to death; who to famine, who to plenty; who to riches, who to poverty; who to birth, who to barrenness. In God's hands is the destiny of each human being, as she sings, "The Lord will judge the ends of the earth." This she knows from experience. Unlike Peninna, Elkana, and

Eli, Chana sees the divine in both the personal and the national.

In the closing phrase of the body of the song, she points to the reason why this is so: God is the Creator who has not abandoned the earth. God establishes the very foundation upon which He set the created earth. God, by the continuity of creatorship, continues to be involved in the world and its ongoing human affairs.

In the climax, Chana summarizes and prophesies: God will watch over the faithful, and the wicked will be undone. There is purpose to life; the apparent triumph of the mighty and the wicked will not long endure. No person will prevail by human power. God does this, she tells us, because God judges all to the very ends of the earth. Now comes the prophecy: Because God manages human affairs, and history has a purpose, Chana prophesies that her son, Shemuel, will designate and anoint the king — David — to whom God will give strength and power. God will raise up the pride of David, His anointed one. Chana translates her experience of personal salvation into an epic of national redemption. Her song's crescendo prepares the way for the basic theme of the Book of Shemuel: the leadership of her son the prophet and the ascendancy to the throne of two unlikely candidates of humble origin — Sha'ul and David.

Chana's designation as a prophetess is affirmed by the rabbis.

תלמוד בבלי מסכת מגילה דף יד עמוד א

שבע נביאות מאן נינהו? שרה, מרים, דבורה, חנה, אביגיל, חולדה, ואסתר.... חנה דכתיב ותתפלל חנה ותאמר עלץ לבי בה' רמה קרני בה'

There are seven prophetesses, who are they? Sarah, Miriam, Devorah, Chana, Avigayil, Hulda, and Esther. Chana [is a prophetess], as it is written: And Chana prayed and said, "My heart exults in the Lord, my horn is exalted in the Lord" (Megilla 14a).

Chana is a prophetess. Her song is the overture to the Book of Shemuel. Her song foretells what will happen in the book named for her son. He brings to reality what his mother sang.

שמואל א פרק ב (ח) מֵקִים מֵעָפָר דָּל מֵאַשְׁפֹּת יָרִים אֶבְיוֹן לְהוֹשִׁיב עִם־נְדִיבִים וְכִסֵּא כָבוֹד יַנְחִלֵם.

He raises the poor from the dust, lifts up the needy from the dunghill, setting them with nobles, granting them seats of honor (I Shemuel 2:8).

Raising up the poor and the lowly from the dust heap and seating them on the throne of honor is the theme of the Book of Shemuel. This is what her son, the prophet Shemuel, will do in identifying and anointing Sha'ul and then David as kings over Israel. The last verse in her song reads:

שמואל א פרק ב (י) ...וְיִתֶּן־עֹז לְמַלְכּוֹ וְיָרֵם קֶרֶן מְשִׁיחוֹ:

He will give power to His king, and triumph to His anointed one (I Shemuel 2:10).

This is realized in God's unconditional promise of the monarchy to David.

שמואל ב פרק כב (נא) מִגְדּוֹל יְשׁוּעוֹת מַלְכּוֹ וְעֹשֶׂה חֶסֶד לִמְשִׁיחוֹ לְדָוִד וּלְזַרְעוֹ עַד עוֹלָם:

Tower of victory to His king, who deals graciously with His anointed, with David and his offspring evermore (II Shemuel 22:51).

תהלים פרק קלב (יז) שָׁם אַצְמִיחַ קֶרֶן לְדָוִד עָרַכְתִּי נֵר לִמְשִׁיחִי:

There I will make a horn sprout for David; I have prepared a lamp for My anointed one (Tehilim 132:17).

Chana's epic thanksgiving song to God inspires Israel's sweetest singer, David, the future author of most of the psalms. Thus, Chana's song is not limited to just the first day of Rosh HaShana. We hear its echoes and refrains throughout the prayerful year. The collection of psalms known as Hallel, "praise" (Psalms 113-118), is recited on the three pilgrimage festivals; on each day of Hanuka; and on Rosh Hodesh, the celebration of the new cycle of the moon. Its opening paragraph is reminiscent of Chana's life and song.

תהלים פרק קיג (א) הַלְלוּ יָהּ הַלְלוּ עַבְדֵי יְקֹוָק הַלְלוּ אֶת־שֵׁם יְקֹוָק: (ב) יְהִי
שֵׁם יְקֹוָק מְבֹרָךְ מֵעַתָּה וְעַד־עוֹלָם: (ג) מִמִּזְרַח־שֶׁמֶשׁ עַד־מְבוֹאוֹ מְהֻלָּל שֵׁם
יְקֹוָק: (ד) רָם עַל־כָּל־גּוֹיִם יְקֹוָק עַל הַשָּׁמַיִם כְּבוֹדוֹ: (ה) מִי כַּיקֹוָק אֱלֹהֵינוּ
הַמַּגְבִּיהִי לָשָׁבֶת: (ו) הַמַּשְׁפִּילִי לִרְאוֹת בַּשָּׁמַיִם וּבָאָרֶץ: (ז) מְקִימִי מֵעָפָר דָּל
מֵאַשְׁפֹּת יָרִים אֶבְיוֹן: (ח) לְהוֹשִׁיבִי עִם־נְדִיבִים עִם נְדִיבֵי עַמּוֹ: (ט) מוֹשִׁיבִי
עֲקֶרֶת הַבַּיִת אֵם־הַבָּנִים שְׂמֵחָה הַלְלוּ־יָהּ:

Halleluja. Praise, O servants of the Lord, praise the Lord's name. May the Lord's name be blessed now and forevermore. From the place the sun rises to where it sets, praised be the name of the Lord. High over all nations, the Lord, over the Heavens His glory. Who is like the Lord our God, who sits high above, who sees down below in the Heavens and on the earth? He raises the poor from the dust, from the dungheap lifts the needy, to seat him among princes, among the princes of his people. He seats the barren woman in her home a happy mother of sons. Halleluja (Tehilim 113).

David, of humble pastoral origins, sits on the throne among princes in fulfillment of the prophecy in Chana's song. He acknowledges her as the barren woman now the happy mother of sons.

At the conclusion of this epic song of thanksgiving, we must pause and look back at what we have heard and seen from Chana at prayer. We witnessed her initial prayer, silence emerging from hardened bitterness and tears. We learned that, as she stood in prayer, Eli the High Priest stood with her and listened as she made a bargain with God for a child vouchsafed by an oath. Following the birth of the child and her return to Shiloh, we listen in and, for millennia, study and celebrate her *shir*, her song. It is as clear as this: Chana is the only person in TaNaKh who presents God with a request, and when that request is granted, sings a song of thanksgiving.

We have many songs of thanksgiving, but none is preceded by a prayerful request. We have many prayerful requests, but none is followed by a thanksgiving song. Chana is a woman saturated by the experience of *tefila*. She is the *mitpalelet*, the praying woman, bar none. She presents prayer in bargain and oath. She presents prayer in thanksgiving.

At the outset, we noted that national saga begins in personal and familial experience. Israel's barrenness is embodied in Chana. Israel's redemption is realized through her service of the heart. Chana moves from *tefila* to *shira*, from plea to thanksgiving, from personal petition to intercession, and from bargain to public song. The key to her thanksgiving song lies in the acknowledgment that her personal experience is the realization of the universal in her particular circumstance. Thus, unlike so very many today who traffic in narcissism, Chana celebrates the universality of God's relationship to all humanity as the key belief that informs her life. She realizes that her suffering is not at all about herself.

In TaNaKh, other moments of triumph and redemption are celebrated with an epic poem of thanksgiving. These are all national experiences. Chana's poem is the only one composed for a personal, individual experience. Can Chana's song be included in the roster of national epic poems? The first, and possibly best known, is the epic song that Moshe and Israel sang at the sea. In commenting on this the classic Ta'anitic Midrash for the Book of Shemot, Mekhilta de Rabbi Ishmael lists ten such epic songs.

מכילתא דרבי ישמעאל בשלח מסכתא דשירה פרשה א
את השירה הזאת וכי שירה אחת היא והלא עשר שירות הן, הראשונה שנאמרה במצרים שנ' השיר יהיה לכם כליל התקדש חג וגו' (ישעיה ל כט), השנייה שנאמרה על הים שנ' אז ישיר משה השלישית שנאמרה על הבאר שנ' אז ישיר ישראל (במדבר כא יז), הרביעית שאמר משה שנ' ויהי ככלות משה לכתוב את דברי השירה הזאת (דברים לא כד), החמישית שאמר יהושע שנ' אז ידבר יהושע לה' ביום תת ה' וגו' (יהושע י יב), הששית שאמרה דבורה וברק שנ' ותשר דבורה וברק בן אבינועם (שופטים ה א), השביעית שאמר דוד שנ' וידבר דוד לה' את דברי השירה הזאת (ש"ב =שמואל ב'= כב א), השמינית שאמר שלמה שנאמר מזמור שיר חנוכת הבית לדוד (תהלים ל א)... התשיעית שאמר יהושפט שנ' ויועץ יהושפט ויעמד משוררים לה' מהללים בהדרת קדש בצאת לפני החלוץ אומר הודו לה' כי לעולם חסדו (דה"ב =דברי הימים ב'= כ כא)... העשירית לעתיד לבא שנ' שירו לה' שיר חדש תהלתו מקצה הארץ (ישעיה מב י)...

"This song [epic poem]" … and is this the only song in TaNaKh? Are there not ten such songs or epic poems? The first was uttered in Egypt, as it is written, You shall have a song like the song sung in the night when the feast was hallowed (Isaiah 30:29). The second song was uttered at the sea, as it is written, Then sang Moshe … (Shemot 15:1). The third song was uttered at the well, as it is written, Then sang Israel … (Bamidbar 21:17). The fourth was the one Moshe uttered, as it is written, And it came to pass when Moshe concluded writing … (Devarim 31:24). The fifth song was uttered by Joshua (on the defeat of the Amorite kings), as it is written, Then spoke Joshua to the Lord … (Joshua 10:12). The sixth was uttered by Devorah and Barak, as it is written, Then sang Devorah and Barak, the son of Avinoam … (Judges 5:1). The seventh was the one David uttered, as it is written, And David spoke unto the Lord the words of this song (II Shemuel 22:1). The eighth was the one uttered by Solomon, as it is written, A psalm, a song at the dedication of the House of David (Tehilim 30:1). The ninth was the one Yehoshaphat uttered, as it is written, And when he had taken counsel with the people, he appointed those who should sing unto the Lord and praise in the beauty of holiness (II Chronicles 20:21). And it continues, Give thanks to the Lord, for His mercy endures forever (II Chronicles 20:21). The tenth song is the one for the future time, as it is written, Sing unto the Lord a new song and His praise from the end of the earth (Isaiah 42:10); it is also written, Sing to the Lord a new song and His praise in the assembly of the saints (Tehilim 149:1) (Mekhilta de Rabbi Yismael, Tractate Shira 1).

That the rabbis identify ten such epic poems, presented at moments of great victory or transition, is not surprising. Ten is a complete set, a microcosm number. For example, the fundamental principles of Judaism, as presented in the Torah, are captured in the Ten Principles (more popularly known as the Ten Commandments). As this *midrash* is handed down from one generation to the next, it emerges again in a late *targum*, a poetic translation of the Torah into Aramaic. The Targum often moves beyond translation to commentary. The *targum* on Shir HaShirim (Song of Songs), in receiving this *midrash*, and studying it, makes several changes.

שירין ותשבחן דאמר שלמה נביא מלכא דישראל ברוח קודשא קדם ריבון כל עלמא ה׳ עשרתי שירתא אתאמרו בעלמא והדא שירתא משבחא מן כולהון: שירתא קדמיתא אמר אדם בזמן דאשתביק ליה חובתיה ואתא יומא דשבתא ואגין עלוהי פתח פומיה ואמר מזמור שיר ליומא דשבתא: שירתא תניתא אמר משה עם בני ישראל בזמן דבזע להון מרי שמיא ית ימא דסוף פתחו כולהון פומהון כחדא ואמרו שירתא דהכין כתיב אז ישיר משה ובני ישראל: שירתא תליתיתא אמרו בני ישראל בזמן דאתיהיבת להון בירא דמיא דהכין כתיב בכין שבח משה ובני ישראל ית תושבחתא: שירתא רביעיתא אמר משה כד אתא זמניה למפטר מן עלמא ואוכח בה ית עמא בית ישראל דהכין כתיב אציתו שמיא ואמליל: שירתא חמישיתא אמר יהושע בר נון כד אגיח קרבא בגבעון וקמו ליה שמשא וסיהרא תלתין ושית שען ופסקו מלמימר שירתא פתח פומיה ואמר שירתא דהכין כתיב כדין שבח יהושע קדם ה׳: שירתא שתיתיתא אמר ברק ודבורה ביומא דמסר ה׳ ית סיסרא וית משריתיה ביד בני ישראל דהכין כתיב ושבחת דבורה וברק בר אבינועם: שירתא שביעיתא אמרת חנה בזמן דאתיהיב לה בר מן קדם ה׳ דהכין כתיב וצליאת חנה ברוח נבואה: שירתא תמיניתא אמר דוד מלכא דישראל על כל ניסא דעבד ליה ה׳ פתח פומיה ואמר שירה דהכין כתיב ושבח דויד בנבואה קדם ה׳: שירתא תשיעיתא אמר שלמה

מלכא דישראל ברוח קודשא קדם ריבון כל עלמא ה׳: שירתא עשיריתא עתידין למימר בני ישראל בעדן דיפקון מן גלותהון דהכין כתיב ומפרש על ידי ישעיה שירה הדין יהי לכון לחדוא כלילא יתקדש חגא דפסחא וחדות לבא בעמא דאזלין לאתחזאה קדם ה׳ תלת זמנין בשתא במיני זמר וקל טבלא למיעל לטורא דה׳ למפלח קדם תקיפא דישראל: (תרגום ירושלמי שיר השירים)

Ten songs were uttered in the world, and this song (Solomon's Song of Songs) is superior to all of them. The first song Adam uttered when his sin against God was remitted and the Sabbath day came and shielded him; he opened his mouth and declared, "A Song for the Sabbath Day ..." The second song Moshe uttered, together with all Israel at the time that the Master of Heaven split the Sea of Reeds. All of them opened their mouths with one voice and uttered the song, of which it is said, "Then Moshe and the Children of Israel sang ..." The third song the children of Israel uttered when they were granted the well of water (in the desert), of which it is written, "Moshe and the children of Israel offered praise." The fourth song Moshe uttered when it came time for him to depart from this world. Thereby he reproved the whole House of Israel. As it says, "Listen O Heavens, and I will speak ..." The fifth song Joshua son of Nun uttered when he made war in Givon as they (the sun and the moon) stood still for him for 36 hours, and ceased offering song (before God). Joshua opened his mouth and uttered this song, as it is written, "And thus did Joshua offer praise before God ..." The sixth song was uttered by Barak and Devorah on the day that God handed over Sisera and his armies to the hands of the Children of Israel. This is what is written, "And Devorah and Barak, son of Avinoam, sang ..." The seventh song Chana uttered when a son was given to her from God. This is what is written, "And Chana prayed in the spirit of prophecy." The eighth song was uttered by David, king of Israel, for all the miracles that God performed for him. He opened his mouth and uttered a song, as it is written, "And David gave praise before God in a state of prophecy." The ninth song was uttered by Solomon, king of Israel, in the Holy Spirit in the presence of the Master of the Universe. The tenth song the Children of Israel are destined to utter when they come forth from their exile, as it is written and explained by Isaiah, "This song will be one of gladness for you, as on the night when the Passover festival is hallowed; there shall be rejoicing as when they march to appear before God three times a year with many musical instruments and bells to go up to the Mountain of God to worship before the Mighty One of Israel" (Targum, Song of Songs 1:1).

The Ten Epic Songs of TaNaKh: Two Versions

	Mekhilta	**Targum**
1	Pesakh in Egypt	Adam's first Shabbat
2	Moshe at the sea	Moshe at the sea
3	The well in the desert	The well in the desert
4	Moshe's valedictory	Moshe's valedictory
5	Joshua's victory	Joshua's victory
6	Devorah's victory	Devorah's victory
7	David's valedictory	Chana's thanksgiving
8	Solomon at Temple dedication	David's valedictory
9	Yehoshafat's victory	Solomon at Temple dedication
10	Messianic era	Messianic era

As the chart shows, the Targum makes two substitutions in the ten epic songs of Israel. It deletes the first one. It does not include the songs of praise that Israel must have surely offered on that first Passover night, that first night of freedom. It is easy for the Targum to do this. The Passover ritual was held family by family. All Israel was not gathered together. Furthermore, including their song of thanksgiving on that Passover night relies on the use of a verse from Isaiah. It is not mentioned in the narrative of that night in Shemot 12.

The Targum also omits the song of Yehoshafat, likely because the events celebrated by the king did not have lasting consequence for Israel. The Targum adds two heretofore unmentioned songs. To universalize the experience of epic songs presented to the Lord at great moments of celebration or transition, the Targum adds the song that Adam sang in praise of God for the gift of the Sabbath. For our purposes, what is noteworthy is that the Targum includes the thanksgiving prayer song of Chana. The song of Adam, as the father of humanity, is not just of Jewish national consequence, but of universal significance. Chana's song, however, is the declaration of thanksgiving of one tormented woman in praise of God who has answered her prayers by giving her a child.

Why is this, the only song of thanksgiving for an individual experience, included in the roster? From the very outset, Chana, in promising the child to the service of God and Israel, made of her personal experience a national drama. It seems that the Targum includes this in its list of ten consequential national epic poems because Chana's son, Shemuel, will inaugurate the monarchy of the House of David that will unify the Twelve Tribes of Israel and establish the Temple in Jerusalem.

This *targum* raises an important question that leads to a bold transformation. Most of the epic songs enumerated in this *targum* begin with either the noun or verb form of *shir* ("song" or "epic poem.") The Song of Chana begins with the verb *vatitpaleyl*, "and Chana prayed." It is clear in the plain reading of the text that Chana is praying as an individual who is giving thanks to God for answering her plea for a child. The noun and verb forms of *shir* appear to be reserved for epic songs that commemorate national experiences. Including Chana's prayer in a list with other national epic songs, the Targum transforms Chana's prayer into a national epic song. Until the Targum it was referred to as *Tefilat Chana,* the prayer of Chana. After the Targum, in common Jewish parlance the prayer of Chana is known as *Shirat Chana,* the Song of Chana. The Targum did this because it is Chana who brings Shemuel onto the stage of Jewish history. He prepares the way for the unification of the Twelve Tribes into a nation through King David. As we have shown above, Chana's prophecy foretells this. Thus, it makes perfect sense for the Targum to view her personal *tefila* as a national *shir.*

God's judgment upon Chana does not end with the birth of Shemuel.

שמואל א פרק ב (יח) וּשְׁמוּאֵל מְשָׁרֵת אֶת־פְּנֵי יְקֹוָק נַעַר חָגוּר אֵפוֹד בָּד: (יט)
וּמְעִיל קָטֹן תַּעֲשֶׂה־לּוֹ אִמּוֹ וְהַעַלְתָה לוֹ מִיָּמִים יָמִימָה בַּעֲלוֹתָהּ אֶת־אִישָׁהּ
לִזְבֹּחַ אֶת־זֶבַח הַיָּמִים: (כ) וּבֵרַךְ עֵלִי אֶת־אֶלְקָנָה וְאֶת־אִשְׁתּוֹ וְאָמַר יָשֵׂם
יְקֹוָק לְךָ זֶרַע מִן־הָאִשָּׁה הַזֹּאת תַּחַת הַשְּׁאֵלָה אֲשֶׁר שָׁאַל לַיקֹוָק וְהָלְכוּ
לִמְקֹמוֹ: (כא) כִּי־פָקַד יְקֹוָק אֶת־חַנָּה וַתַּהַר וַתֵּלֶד שְׁלֹשָׁה־בָנִים וּשְׁתֵּי בָנוֹת
וַיִּגְדַּל הַנַּעַר שְׁמוּאֵל עִם־יְקֹוָק:

Shemuel was engaged in the service of the Lord as an attendant, girded with a linen ephod. His mother would also make a little robe for him and bring it up to him every year, when she made the pilgrimage with her husband to offer the annual sacrifice. Eli would bless Elkana and his wife, saying, "May the Lord grant you offspring by this woman in place of the loan she made to the Lord." Then they would return home. For the Lord took note of Chana; she conceived and bore three sons and two daughters. Young Shemuel, meanwhile, grew up in the service of the Lord (I Shemuel 2:18-21).

This is not the end of the story of the family of Elkana and Chana. She regularly visits her child, Shemuel, when she goes up to Shilo with Elkana. Eli the High Priest, who once thought her a drunkard, now gives her a blessing that she will have more children, because she has "loaned" this first child to God. God hears the blessing of Eli. Chana soon births three sons and two daughters. We then learn something unheard of in any other figure in TaNaKh: The child Shemuel grows up with God. Remember that Moshe grows up in Pharaoh's palace. Shemuel's childhood schoolroom, his playground, is the Mishkan. His youthful companion is the Kadosh Barukh Hu.

Her oath fulfilled, Chana witnesses her contract and dream, Shemuel in the Mishkan. She is the *mitpalelet*, the intercessor. She has the confidence and sense of justice that only authenticity purchases. She is the woman who entered the Mishkan.

The rabbis are with her every step of the way. They transport her from the ancient Mishkan to the contemporary *siddur,* order of prayer. In the teachings of the rabbis, she takes her stand in the synagogue then and now.

PART 2
The Rabbinic Portrait of Chana

1

Chana and the Practice of Prayer

If this were a novel, our story of Chana would now end. But this is the Bible, whose dramas have a life and career that flourish long after the close of the book. This is the beginning of learning and imagining. A narrative in the Bible is addressed to the faithful reader throughout the ages. Its purpose is the provocation of the learner. It seeks, it demands a response: What does this narrative teach me about myself and my purpose? In each biblical narrative, the reader seeks meaning and guidance to life's purposes and mysteries. Once read and known, the text is now available to be explored for limitless ideas and life instructions.

Foremost among the Bible's readers are the rabbis, the great authors of the Midrash, Mishna, and Talmud. The rabbis flourished from approximately 30 BCE to the sixth century. Along with Eli the High Priest, the rabbis are present when Chana enters the Sanctuary and begins to pray. They, too, are captivated by the portrait of this praying woman. Through Chana they carefully study the ways of prayer and mold the Jewish people into a praying community. Through Chana, the rabbis treat the basic and the complex issues and challenges faced in prayer.

What does the behavior of Chana teach us about the practice of prayer? The Torah instructs the Jewish people to pray. The Torah does not provide the texts or the ways of prayer. The rabbis do that by composing and fashioning the *siddur*. But how is a Jew to use the *siddur*? The rabbis turn to Chana to instruct the Jewish people in the culture of prayer.

The rabbis are intrigued by Chana's person in prayer. Like Eli, they have never quite seen such a person, let alone such a woman. The biblical text is sparse. There is much about Chana's recorded behavior in the biblical text that cries out: Portray me! Pursue my meaning! The rabbis set themselves the task of presenting the behavior and exploring the inner life of Chana in rich detail. They give us her prayerful portrait that we might pray.

The rabbis turn to gaze upon Chana to learn the practice of *tefila*, as they teach prayer to the Jewish people. They watch her every gesture as intently as Eli did long ago. They study Chana in order to explain a particular passage in the Mishna.

This *mishna*, which begins the fifth chapter of Tractate Berakhot in the Talmud Bavli, does not deal with prayer in general. It refers to only one prayer, the Amida (Standing Prayer) — a *tefila* known as prayer in its essence. The first four chapters in Tractate Berakhot present and analyze the Shema and the morning prayers that precede the Amida, also known as the Shmoneh Esreh (Eighteen Berakhot). In the prayer book, as it has come down to us from the rabbis of the Talmud, the praying Jew walks a path before approaching God in the austere, standing silence of the Amida. First, *berakhot*, "acknowledgments," are made for the essentials of life and the unique features of Jewish belief. This is followed by verses largely taken from the Book of Psalms, culminating in the recitation of the promise made to Avraham and Moshe's Song at the Sea. This section begins and ends with acknowledgment of the Psalms of David, which make it possible for a Jew to praise God. After all, the words of the ancient ones in deep intimacy with God serve us better than any we might compose ourselves.

This is followed by the Shema and its surrounding *berakhot*, which frame it. The Shema is preceded by exalted and intense appreciation of God's creatorship; of Israel's imitation of the heavenly sanctification of the name of God; of a prayer for the light of creation to shine upon Zion; and of acknowledgment of God's great love for Israel as reflected in the gift of the Torah. The Shema is followed by gratitude for the redemption from slavery in Egypt. It is only at this point, after acknowledging God's many unearned gifts, that a Jew can rise and enter into the presence of God to present the Amida, his or her petitions in the whispered voice of Chana.

The Tractate Berakhot is devoted to the study and presentation of the *halakhot*, the ways of *tefila* and *berakhot*, the range of occasional blessings for food and the varieties of human experience. The first three chapters of Berakhot deal with the recitation of the Shema and its constituent three paragraphs from the Torah. The fourth chapter turns from the Shema, by way of thanksgiving for redemption, to the Amida, the whispered devotional petition of the faithful Jew. The fifth chapter is an immersion in the inner life experience of *tefila*. In this case, *tefila* refers not to prayer in general, but rather to the Shmoneh Esreh, the standing, whispered prayer of the Eighteen Berakhot.

We learn in a *mishna*:

מסכת ברכות דף ל עמוד ב משנה אין עומדין להתפלל אלא מתוך כובד ראש. חסידים הראשונים היו שוהין שעה אחת ומתפללין, כדי שיכוונו לבם לאביהם שבשמים...

One may not stand and initiate prayer save from a posture of gravity and submission. There is a tradition that the early pietists would wait one hour in order to reach the solemn frame of mind appropriate for prayer and then pray so that they would focus their hearts toward their father in Heaven ... (Mishna Berakhot 30b).

The Mishna, like all codes, is dry and matter-of-fact. Its purpose is to establish rules for Jewish behavior. The rabbis have to bring the code to life, to animate it with inspiration, in order to teach the Jewish people how to put it into practice. The Mishna's requirement and standard for prayer is difficult to teach and harder to implement. The call of the Mishna is two words: *koved rosh* (literally "heavy head," or "seriousness"). This is a call not to action, but to a state of mind and heart.

The Mishna usually instructs behavior and procedure. This is an exceptional case. Inner life experiences are generally left to Agada. How to build a *sukka* or bake *matza* is easy to instruct. But in order to stand before God in *tefila,* one has to be infused with a sense of the gravity of the experience. How will the rabbis teach an inner life experience, a state of mind? How will they present this concept in an instructive and inspiring way? There is only one way: by example. Certain ideas are book taught and book learned. Prayer, like human relationships, is learned mimetically.

The question is: Whose actual *tefila* practice serves as an instructive example of the inner life experience required of a Jew in prayer? There are many people in the TaNaKh who pray. Eliyahu prays. We have his words, but that is all. Moshe prays quite often on behalf of the Jewish people. We have his words, but not the prayerful experience of his inner life. His prayer conduct, reflected in a posture or mood or facial expression, is not described in the Torah. There is only one person in TaNaKh for whom we have a comprehensive description of the inner life in prayer and the way that spirit is plainly seen by an observer or a student of prayer. It is Chana. For a faithful Jew to come forward and stand in the presence of God in *tefila* is to mimic Chana. It is Chana at prayer whom the rabbis present that we ourselves might come into His presence and speak with Him.

The rabbis turn to Chana to teach *darkei tefila*, the "pathways of prayer." Chana is the *mishna* brought to life. The rabbis see in Chana something so remarkable that they use a word associated with no other person's religious experience in order to portray *koved rosh.* The Talmud in Berakhot 31a reads:

אמר רב המנונא: כמה הלכתא **גברוותא** איכא למשמע מהני קראי דחנה:

Rav Hamnuna said, "How many **powerful and important** *halakhot* can be derived from these verses [of the prayer and life] of Chana?" (Berakhot 31a).

Chana embodies the power and importance of prayer.

Rav Hamnuna then presents the following *halakhot*, practices modeled on Chana for proper conduct in *tefila*.

ברכות דף לא עמוד א וחנה היא מדברת על לבה   מכאן למתפלל צריך שיכוין לבו. רק שפתיה נעות   מכאן למתפלל שיחתוך בשפתיו. וקולה לא ישמע   מכאן, שאסור להגביה קולו בתפלתו. ויחשבה עלי לשכרה   מכאן, ששכור אסור להתפלל...

Rav Hamnuna said: How many powerful and important halakhot can be derived from these verses of the prayer **of Chana?** As it says: "And Chana spoke in her heart, only her lips moved and her voice could not be heard, so Eli thought her to be drunk" (I Shemuel 1:13). The Gemara elaborates: **From** that which is stated **here**: **"And Chana spoke in her heart,"** the *halakha* that **one who prays must enunciate** the words **with his lips,** not only contemplate them in his heart, is derived. **From** that which is written **here: "And her voice could not be heard,"** the *halakha* that **one is forbidden to raise his voice in his *Amida* prayer** as it must be recited quietly. From the continuation of the verse **here: "So Eli thought her to be drunk,"** the *halakha* that a **drunk person is forbidden to pray.** That is why he rebuked her (Berakhot 31a, Koren Edition).

These are the *halakhot*, the requisite behaviors derived from Chana's conduct during *tefila*.

1. The praying person must be intently devotional in his or her heart.

2. One who prays must clearly articulate the words of the prayer with his or her lips. It is not enough to think them and intend them in the heart.

3. One is forbidden to raise his or her voice during the silent Amida.

4. A drunken person is forbidden to pray.

The second and third *halakhot* are bound up one with the other. The Jew in prayer must clearly articulate each word. Prayer, after all, is serious discourse. Words spoken in conviction and devotion to the one God must not be merely thought or hastily considered. The praying person must be able to hear his or her own words. At the same time, this is a private conversation. The self and God are the only audience for this prayer; thus, as the third *halakha* states, the praying person is forbidden to raise his or her voice during the silent Amida. This is the model Chana establishes. It is the intimate and private relationship that Chana has with God that presents the whispered prayer.

Chana's whispered prayer sets precedent for the rabbis.

תלמוד בבלי מסכת ברכות דף כד עמוד ב המשמיע קולו בתפלתו הרי זה מקטני אמנה.

One who sounds his voice during the Amida prayer is of little faith (Berakhot 24b).

The Midrash makes a similar comment.

מדרש אגדה (בובר) דברים פרשת ואתחנן פרק ו ודברת בם. בם ולא בתפלה, שקרית שמע צריכה לאמרה בדיבור עז כדי שישמעו, אבל תפלה בלחש, כשם שעשתה חנה:

... *and speak of them* ...(Devarim 6:7). "Speak of them ..." (the recitation of the Shema), but not so for *tefila* (the Amida). For the recitation of the Shema has to be articulated in bold speech so that it is heard, but *tefila* (the Amida) [is to be recited] in a whisper following the practice of Chana (Midrash Agada [Buber] Devarim Va'Etkh'anan, 6).

For the rabbis, the description of the *halakhot* for prayer is necessary but insufficient. Once they present requisite behaviors for prayer based on the conduct of Chana, the rabbis invite us to join as they watch and study Chana at prayer. Her drama is presented in a text book — the biblical Book of Shemuel. The rabbis transform Chana into a person whose very life and conduct become a teaching text. Chana is a text person. They want us to subject Chana's stance and words and inner life to close reading and study. They present her as an example that embodies the depth and complexity of seeking relationship in conversation with God. The rabbinic portrait of Chana in prayer encompasses a wide range of ideas and gestures. It moves from the simplicity of reasoned need and request to demand, then to claim, then to confrontation itself.

2

The Normalcy of Prayer

We read in the Midrash:

פסיקתא רבתי (איש שלום) פיסקא-מג כי פקד ה' את חנה
ואף חנה על שהייתה תדירה להיות עולה ומתפללת בבית המקדש ומתחננת לפני הקדוש ברוך הוא שמע תפילתה ופקדה, מניין, ממה שקרינן בענין כי פקד ה' [את] חנה.

And Chana, because she regularly went up and prayed in the Beit HaMikdash and sought favor and compassion in the presence of the Holy One, blessed be He, He heard her prayer and He judged her. As it said: For God has remembered Chana (Pesikta Rabbati 43).

Chana has earned the right to bring the most important matters of life to God in her unique way. She is a regular. One cannot present ultimate demand of God or person absent a highly developed relationship. Familiarity breeds commitment. Standing in the eyes of God is the reward of regularity.

The rabbis deploy Chana to deal with a basic question about the seeming impossibility of prayer.

תלמוד ירושלמי מסכת ברכות פרק ט
ראה כמה הוא גבוה מעולמו ואדם נכנס לבית הכנסת ועומד אחורי העמוד ומתפלל בלחישה והקב"ה מאזין את תפלתו. שנאמר [שמואל א א יג] וחנה היא מדברת על לבה רק שפתיה נעות וקולה לא ישמע והאזין הקב"ה את תפילתה. וכן כל בריותיו שנאמר [תהילים קב א] תפילה לעני כי יעטף כאדם המשיח באוזן חבירו והוא שומע. וכי יש לך אלוה קרוב מזה שהוא קרוב לבריותיו כפה לאוזן.

> Mark well how exalted God is above His world, and yet a person enters the synagogue and stands before the reader's table and prays in a whisper, and the Holy One, blessed be He, hears him. As it says: And Chana spoke from her heart. Indeed, her lips moved but her voice was not heard and the Holy One, blessed be He, hearkened to her prayer. And so too for all His creatures, as it says: a prayer of the tormented, when he is faint (Tehilim 102:1), like a person who converses in his friend's ear and he hears. And is there a God closer than this (God) who is as close to His creatures as the mouth to the ear? (Talmud Yerushalmi Berakhot 9).

This passage from the Talmud Yerushalmi deals with a question that, if not addressed, threatens to make prayer impossible. God is utterly exalted, beyond time and space. What is it that can cross this chasm between the finite human and the infinite exalted God? The rabbis respond in a naturalistic way. They are keen observers of human experience. A person enters and takes a position in the synagogue. The person prays in a whisper. God hearkens and listens to the prayer. The answer of the rabbis is self-evident. It is born of common human experience. God is surely exalted. The human is not. The human presents *tefila.* God hears and accepts.

The human comes to the synagogue, positions herself before God, and prepares to have conversation with God. God, as exalted as He is, will listen. Is there such a person? The rabbis know this from the experience of Chana. Ever so naturally, she stood up and came forth from her fasting and hunger and tears. She walked to and entered the Mishkan, and stood in the presence of God. She did this without preparation or ceremony or permission from any authority. What she did is ever so normal for the faithful Jew. She went to talk with God. The devotional life experience of Chana in prayer is the proof-text for the rabbis that sincerely offered human prayer will be heard by the one exalted God.

In Chana's stance in the Mishkan, the rabbis imagine themselves and the Jewish people at prayer. They recognize her. They know this woman. Her prayer conduct is familiar.

She is doing what they and the Jewish people have been doing since the destruction of the Second Temple.

When the Temple in Jerusalem was destroyed by the Romans in the year 70, the Jewish people confronted a crisis that, if not addressed, would have — Heaven forefend! — brought an end to Israel's sacred life with the Almighty. The Beit HaMikdash, Temple, was the shared House of God and Israel. Situated atop Mount Moriah in Jerusalem, it was the place to which Jews in the Land of Israel and the Diaspora would make pilgrimage three times a year — at Pesakh, Shavuot, and Sukkot. All eyes, all hearts, were focused on the Temple as the place in which God and Israel were reconciled, the place to which every Jew could come to receive atonement for sin and reconciliation with God. It was a shared house, a place in which God and Israel lived. This is poignantly expressed in the Temple Dedicatory speech of King Solomon.

The house was destroyed. What would replace it? The service of God was realized in the presentation of all manner of *korbanot*, animal and cereal offerings, without which there seemed to be no means of forgiveness and reconciliation. One cannot overstate the crisis to Judaism and the Jewish people brought on by the cessation of animal offerings, the destruction of the shared house, and the end of the priesthood. In this moment of great crisis, the rabbis reached back to the experience of Israel in the desert, to the First and Second Temple periods, to the Psalms of David. They realized that what was lost with the end of *korbanot* could be regained and expressed in the service of the heart, in *tefila*. In the years following the destruction of the Temple, the *siddur*, the ordered way of prayer, was developed by the rabbis. Both the synagogue and the Jewish home became successors to the Temple, and *tefila* became the successor to animal offerings. Deprived of animal offerings, the rabbis understood well the words of the Prophet Hoshea.

הושע פרק יד (ג) קְחוּ עִמָּכֶם דְּבָרִים וְשׁוּבוּ אֶל־יְקֹוָק אִמְרוּ אֵלָיו כָּל־תִּשָּׂא
עָוֺן וְקַח־טוֹב וּנְשַׁלְּמָה פָרִים שְׂפָתֵינוּ׃

Take words with you and return to the Lord. Say to Him: Forgive all guilt and accept what is good; instead of bulls we will pay the offering of our lips (Hoshea 14:3).

Prayer for animal offering, the synagogue for the Temple. In the decades following the year 70, Rabban Gamliel composed and organized the thrice daily-recited Amida, Standing Prayer. The Amida is prayer in its essence. It presents to God request for personal and national need.

The two classic weekday Amidot — Shaharit and Mincha — are in corresponding compensation for the *Korban Tamid Shel Shaharit* and *Korban Tamid Shel Bein Ho'Arbayim*, the regular morning and late afternoon offerings in the Temple.

The Amida consists of eighteen blessings, to which a nineteenth is later added. For our purposes, we will survey the initial structure of eighteen. Form follows function in liturgy and literature, as well as in architecture. The purpose and meaning of the Amida is presented in its structure.

I. Praise: The Opening Three Blessings

a. Avot (Patriarchs)

This *berakhah* answers the question: Who are we to talk to God? The answer is: As the children of the patriarchs, we are members of God's intimate family.

b. Gevurot (Powers)

This *berakhah* answers the question: Who is God to whom we should pray? The answer is: He is the one who has the power to resurrect the dead, for inherent in the power to create is the power to bring life to the lifeless.

c. Kedushat Hashem (Sanctification of the Name)

This *berakhah* answers the question: Now that we know who we are and who God is, what is the nature of the relationship? The answer is: God and Israel share in *kedusha*; as God is *kadosh*, "sacred," so is Israel. This blessing, which sanctifies the name of God, establishes the critical link on which prayer is based. Parallel to God's sanctity is Israel's sanctity. Israel is the sacred people who know the sacred name. Because they know the sacred name, they are intimate with God.

II. Personal and National Petition: The Middle Twelve

a. The First Six

Personal petitions for wisdom, repentance, forgiveness, relief from suffering, healing, livelihood

b. The Second Six

National petitions centered on redemption, return to Jerusalem, establishment of the instruments of sovereignty, arrival of the Messiah

III. Thanksgiving: The Closing Three Blessings

a. Avodah (Service)

This *berakhah* seeks the restoration of the service in the Temple, which carries with it the residence of the Shekhina in our midst. It answers the question: What is the most efficacious form of prayer?

b. Hoda'ah (Thanksgiving)

This *berakhah* answers the question: Why have we prayed to God? The answer is: He is the source of all life and all blessing.

c. Birkat Kohanim (Priestly Blessing)

This *berakhah,* in either its *sim shalom* or *shalom rav* form, is a contemplative essay upon the priestly blessing. It answers the question: How will the blessings of God, the source of all life, be realized? The answer is: through the light of God's presence, as reflected in *shalom.*

This, the whispered prayer of the Jew who stands before his or her Creator to present needs and requests, is *tefila* in its essence. It is now clear why Hazal align the *berakhot* of the Amida with the verses of Shirat Chana, the epic Thanksgiving Song of Chana. The way Chana prays — facing God, standing at repose, silently moving her lips, her voice unheard yet her words well-articulated for God to hear — is how we ought conduct ourselves during the Amida's recitation.

Who else in TaNaKh turns to God in prayer or intercession in a whispered voice heard solely by God? Chana is surrounded by noise. Wherever she turns, the voices of others fill the air and her ears. Peninna torments her. Elkana advises her. In the sanctuary at Shiloh, she is surrounded by the throngs of people who come to worship. Her own soul is awash with the voice of tears, the voice of bitterness, the voice of despair. Surely her mind is choked with the voices of Peninna's children.

There is one voice she has yet to hear: the voice of her child. Her environment is filled with noise. In the midst of all of this, what do we read? *And Chana prayed upon God and her voice was not heard, for she was speaking to her heart.* In the midst of so much noise, the only way to be heard is to whisper. Whispering is what takes place between two who know each other. Whispering takes place when no exhibitionism or audience is sought. Whispering is the speech of the one who is self-sufficient and whole in one's self. Whispering takes place when the two are alone with each other.

When we are ready to present the Amida, we are expected to conjure the image of Chana at prayer in the Mishkan. The rabbis see something in Chana that they see in no other praying person, man or woman, in TaNaKh. In Chana they encounter a person who by virtue of the inaudible, whispered prayer is in a cocoon-like retreat with the one God. Within the sanctuary of the noisy Mishkan, Chana prays in a state of natural intimacy with God.

With great attention to detail and with public ceremonial ritual, animal offerings are a regular feature of the drama that is the Temple service. Israel's national worship is public. Indeed, the communal nature of such national offerings is central to their efficacy and purpose. The whole people must serve God, and they must do so through their designated agents, the priests, in the central and only sanctuary in Jerusalem. The public witness of all this binds the nation together. Indeed, the same is true for the individual who brings an animal offering. Sometimes reconciliation for the most private and personal of experiences, sin, impurity, or crime takes place in the public arena.

What does Chana do? Into this place of demonstrative national and personal offerings — to the occasional accompaniment of *shofar* and trumpet blasts, the recitation of psalms and other litanies — comes one woman. In pristine silence, she transforms the public Temple into her personal sanctuary. She takes her private place within this universal arena. Among all Israel, God and this one woman meet in the all-encompassing walls of her silence. In so doing, Chana sets the precedent for personal encounter with God through the words of *tefilot* — prayers that have stood us in good stead these 2,000 years.

In the Song of Chana, the rabbis identify parallels for each of the Amida's eighteen *berakhot*. In the text and translation below, each phrase from Chana's song is followed by the corresponding name or theme of the *berakhah* in the Amida. The rabbis employ word parallels to signal a congruence of ideas. Familiarity and similarity, for the rabbis, breed the presentation and explication of great ideas.

ילקוט שמעוני שמואל א רמז פ

ותתפלל חנה, מכאן אנו למדין שנשים חייבות בתפלה שכן חנה היתה מתפללת י"ח ברכות רמה קרני בה' מגן אברהם. ה' ממית ומחיה מחיה המתים. אין קדוש כה' האל הקדוש. כי אל דעות-ה' אתה חונן. ונכשלים (בעונם) אזרו חיל הרוצה בתשובה, מוריד שאול ויעל המרבה לסלוח. שמחתי בישועתך גואל ישראל. מקימי מעפר-דל רופא חולים. שבעים בלחם מברך השנים. רגלי חסידיו ישמור מקבץ נדחי עמו ישראל. ה' ידין אפסי ארץ אוהב צדקה ומשפט. ורשעים בחשך ידמו מכניע זדים. ויתן עוז למלכו בונה ירושלים. וירם קרן משיחו את צמח דוד. ואין צור כאלהינו שומע תפלה. אל תרבו תדברו גבוהה שאותך לבדך ביראה [נעבוד]. יצא עתק מפיכם הטוב שמך ולך נאה להודות. ויתן עוז למלכו עושה השלום. הרי שמונה עשרה ברכות שהתפללה:

In this *midrash* each phrase in the Song of Chana is followed by its counterpart blessing in the Amida and an explanatory note.

And Chana prayed … (I Shemuel 2:1), from this verse we know that women are obligated to pray, because Chana offered the eighteen *berakhot.*

1. I have triumphed through the Lord | (the first *berakhah*) the Shield of Avraham

The phrase "the Shield of Avraham" is found in Genesis 14, following Avraham's successful war campaign to rescue his nephew. The Shield of Avraham is a symbol of triumph over adversity.

2. God deals death and brings life | who brings life to the dead

This berakhah *is an affirmation that life and death are in the hands of the Creator.*

3. There is none as holy as the Lord | God who is holy

Kedusha, *"sanctity," describes the utter uniqueness of the one God.*

4. For He is a God of wisdom | favor us with wisdom

God is the source of wisdom.

5. Those who have stumbled gird themselves with victory | who desires repentance
The rabbis take this phrase as indicative of the stumbling for which the sinner now seeks repentance.

6. God casts down to Sheol and raises up | He is generous to forgive
This phrase focuses on the punishment that awaits the sinner, the descent into Sheol, and God's raising up the sinner who seeks forgiveness.

7. For I rejoice in His salvation | the redeemer of Israel
Delight in God's salvation is expressed in the prayer for God to save Israel from suffering.

8. Who raises up the poor from the dust | who heals His people Israel
This focuses our attention on the poor and God's commitment to relieve them. The parallel berakhah *is for health. The sick person is presented as impoverished.*

9. Those once sated must hire out for bread | who blesses the crop years
The Song of Chana declares that in God's hands are the measure of famine and plenty. The berakhah *seeks years of plentiful crops.*

10. Who watches the footsteps of His righteous ones | who gathers in the dispersed of Israel
God measures and watches over the footsteps, or path, of the righteous. Israel is the righteous nation, dispersed in exile. This is a prayer for God to guide the footsteps of the righteous to be gathered in the Land of Israel.

11. God will judge the ends of the earth | God who loves righteousness and justice
God is acknowledged and praised for being the supreme and perfect judge. This berakhah *affirms God's love of righteousness and justice.*

12. The wicked perish in darkness | God who crushes the wicked
The song describes the fate of the wicked who do not repent. The berakhah *seeks judgment upon those who continue to sin and thus remain wicked.*

13. And strength to His king | who builds Jerusalem
The song predicts that God will give strength to the king who Shemuel will anoint. This is expressed in the berakhah *for the restoration of the Davidic monarchy.*

14. And triumph to His anointed one | who causes the triumph of salvation to blossom
This foretells the ultimate victory of God's anointed one, the Messiah. The berakhah *prays for redemption.*

15. There is no rock like our Lord | who hears all prayer
This berakhah *refers to God's enduring strength, symbolized by the rock. The* berakhah *affirms the utter reliability of God by acknowledging He hears all prayers.*

16. Talk no more with lofty pride | You alone will we serve
The song delivers an admonition to the arrogant. The berakhah *declares that only God, and no human, will we serve.*

17. Let no arrogance cross your lips | Your name is good
The song continues its warning against arrogance. This berakhah *affirms the goodness of God's name. In the presence of God's name one dare not be arrogant.*

18. And He will give strength to His king | who makes peace
The song closes with the prophecy that God will give strength to His chosen king. This final berakhah *presents the great benefit of a righteous king, namely Shalom, wholesomeness and peace.*

(Yalkut Shimon Shemuel I, 80)

In identifying the eighteen *berakhot* of the Amida in the Song of Chana, the rabbis call us to imagine her three times a day. Like many a person of great spirit, Chana teaches the normal and reveals the mysterious. In the Talmud, she is a model for daily prayer and its simple conduct. Simplicity itself is the gift of great minds and persons. We now to turn Chana the religious thinker, who develops her ideas and beliefs in conversation with God. Unlike scholarly theologians, she talks with God not about God.

3

Demand and Claim

For the rabbis, the common and the intense accompany each other. Chana presents simple and profound, normal and dramatic images. Learning is inherent in relationship. As familiarity develops, each party learns something new about the other. Indeed, there are times when one teaches the other something they may not have heretofore known about themselves. In the process of devotional intimacy with God, Chana reveals something new about God. The Talmud turns to an examination of Chana's understandings of God and her relationship with Him. The rabbis teach that she reveals something of the nature of God. In so doing, as with any increase in knowledge of the other, new expectation and demand can be realized.

> תלמוד בבלי מסכת ברכות דף לא עמוד ב ותדר נדר ותאמר ה' צבאות, אמר רבי אלעזר: מיום שברא הקדוש ברוך הוא את עולמו, לא היה אדם שקראו להקדוש ברוך הוא צבאות עד שבאתה חנה וקראתו צבאות.

> And she (Chana) vowed a vow and said, "O Lord of *tzeva'ot*, hosts ..." Rabbi Eleazar said, "From the day that God created His world there was no man who called the Holy One, blessed be He, [God of] *tzeva'ot* until Chana came and called Him Tzeva'ot" (Berakhot 31b).

God's presence in this world is manifest in the name Y-H-V-H and other honorifics. Human understanding of the different names of God reflects different levels of intimacy with and understandings of God. Inherent in the various names are degrees of knowledge about God and experience with Him. This is readily understood by reference to common human circumstance. The phrase *on a first-name basis* indicates friendship. Those we address as *Mr.* or *Ms.* are those with whom we have a formal and somewhat reserved relationship. Sharing special names with certain people, unknown to others, is an indication of love and deep attachment. Not many in TaNaKh coin or reveal a new name for God. Not many in TaNaKh know special, intimate names for God. When Avraham comes into the Land, we are told:

בראשית פרשת לך לך פרק יב (ז) ...וַיִּבֶן־שָׁם מִזְבֵּחַ לַיקֹוָק וַיִּקְרָא בְּשֵׁם יְקֹוָק:

... and he built there an altar to the Lord and called upon the Lord by name (Be-Reshit 12:8).

The most powerful experience of the revelation of a special name of God is, of course, Moshe's.

שמות פרשת וארא פרק ו (ב) וַיְדַבֵּר אֱלֹהִים אֶל־מֹשֶׁה וַיֹּאמֶר אֵלָיו אֲנִי יְקֹוָק: (ג) וָאֵרָא אֶל־אַבְרָהָם אֶל־ יִצְחָק וְאֶל ־יַעֲקֹב בְּאֵל שַׁדָּי וּשְׁמִי יְקֹוָק לֹא נוֹדַעְתִּי לָהֶם:

God spoke to Moshe and said to him, "I am the Lord. I appeared to Avraham, Isaac, and Jacob as El Shaddai, but I did not make Myself known to them by My name Y-H-V-H (Shemot 6:2, 3).

According to the rabbis, Chana, like Moshe, is given the privilege of revealing a unique name of God. God's presence in this world is manifest in His name. Moshe seeks the name of God. God brings His name to reside among Israel.

במדבר פרשת נשא פרק ו (כז) וְשָׂמוּ אֶת שְׁמִי עַל בְּנֵי יִשְׂרָאֵל וַאֲנִי אֲבָרְכֵם:

Thus they shall place My name upon the people of Israel, and I will bless them (Bamidbar 5:27).

A new name of God is the realization of a deeper understanding of Him. What is this name Tzeva'ot? Who is God as revealed in this name? He is the Lord of Hosts. There are three hosts. He is God whom the *malakhim*, the angels or host on high, serve. He is the Master Creator of the host of Heaven — the sun, moon, planets, and stars. He is the God of Israel, the *tzivot hashem*, the community or constellation of God, as in:

שמות פרשת בא פרק יב (מא) וַיְהִי מִקֵּץ שְׁלֹשִׁים שָׁנָה וְאַרְבַּע מֵאוֹת שָׁנָה וַיְהִי בְּעֶצֶם הַיּוֹם הַזֶּה יָצְאוּ כָּל־צִבְאוֹת יְקֹוָק מֵאֶרֶץ מִצְרָיִם׃

... at the end of the 430th year, to the very day, all the *tzivot*, hosts of the Lord, departed from the land of Egypt (Shemot 12:41).

Thus, God is the creator and maintainer, the symphony conductor, of the material and spiritual realms of the Heaven and the Heavens above, and of their earthly constellation, the Jewish people. Chana reveals this aspect of God in her new name for Him. Furthermore, the rabbis take note of her special knowledge in the revelation of this name by declaring that "there was no person" — not even Moshe — before Chana "who called the Holy One, blessed be He, Tzeva'ot, the Lord of Hosts." In prayer lies the possibility of discovery in the divine realm. The revelation of this name is the unique gift of a woman who is, for the rabbis, the exemplar of a *mitpalelet*. The promise of prayer well mastered is greater knowledge of God.

Spiritually equipped for intercession with this new name of God, Chana, according to Rabbi Eleazar, is emboldened.

תלמוד בבלי מסכת ברכות דף לא עמוד ב אמר רבי אלעזר ... אמרה חנה לפני הקדוש ברוך הוא: רבונו של עולם, מכל צבאי צבאות שבראת בעולמך קשה בעיניך שתתן לי בן אחד? משל למה הדבר דומה למלך בשר ודם שעשה סעודה לעבדיו, בא עני אחד ועמד על הפתח, אמר להם: תנו לי

פרוסה אחת! ולא השגיחו עליו; דחק ונכנס אצל המלך. אמר לו: אדוני המלך, מכל סעודה שעשית קשה בעיניך ליתן לי פרוסה אחת?

> Rabbi Eleazar said ... Chana declared in the presence of the Holy One, blessed be He: Sovereign of the universe, from among all the hosts of the hosts that You have created in Your world, is it so difficult in Your eyes to give me one son? A parable: To what is this comparable? To a king who made a feast for his servants, and a poor man came and stood by the door and said to them, "Give me a bite," and no one took any notice of him, so he forced his way into the presence of the king and said to him, "Your Majesty, from all [the food of] the feast that you have made, is it so difficult in your eyes to give me one bite?" (Berakhot 31b).

Rabbi Eleazar, observing Chana as intently as Eli the High Priest, is captivated by her courage and her resolve. He does not see her as a beggar. He gives voice to what she must surely have said to God. He knows that she is standing and not bent on her knees. In standing she is, if one dare say it, on a plane with God — much as Jacob said, "For I have seen God face to face." In this understanding of Chana's posture, Rabbi Eleazar portrays her in frank conversation, indeed demand, of the Sovereign of the Universe. Possessed of a new name of God, she speaks to Him in a voice of soft chastisement. *You have so much. I have nothing. Is it really so difficult for You to give me just a bit of all that You have?* This, too, is typical of Jewish prayer. The humble Jew approaches God in a bold way with plain requests.

This *midrash* has a career. As *midrashim* are studied and handed down from one generation of Hazal to the next, their ideas are developed, their richness grows. By the time this *midrash* from the second generation Amora Rabbi Eleazar (circa mid-third century, Eretz Yisrael) reaches the period when *midrashim* are collected, organized, and presented in anthologies, it had acquired new drama and depth of meaning. The Pesikta Rabbati, which comes to us in its present state from no earlier than the eighth century, gathered and assembled *midrashim* from the literature of Hazal and crafted a *piska*, a unit for Rosh HaShana titled "And God Remembered Chana."

In this *piska* we have an enriched version of Rabbi Eleazar's initial *midrash* in Berakhot from the pen of the Amora Rabbi Yehuda bar Simon. This should not surprise us. Both rabbinic masters are *darshanim*, public preachers. They are master literary and rhetorical artists. When later rabbis receive earlier material, they artfully develop what they have received. Read it carefully, and be on the lookout for the new.

פסיקתא רבתי (איש שלום) פיסקא-מג כי פקד ה' את חנה
ותדור נדר ותאמר ה' צבאות (שמואל א' א' י"א) מהו ה' צבאות, אמר רבי יהודה בר' סימון אמרה חנה לפני הקדוש ברוך הוא רבונו של עולם יש צבא למעלה יש צבא למטה, הצבא של מעלה אינם [לא] אוכלים ולא שותים ולא פרים ורבים ולא מתים אלא חיים לעולם, והצבא שלמטה אוכלים ושותים ופרים ורבים ומתים, ואיני יודעת מאיזו צבא אני, אם משל מעלה או משל מטה, אם מצבא של מעלה אני, לא אהיה לא אוכלת ולא שותית ולא מולידה ולא מתה אלא חיה לעולם כשם שהם חיים לעולם, ואם מצבא של מטה אני, אהא אוכלת ושותית ומולידה ומתה כשם שהם אוכלים ושותים ופרים ורבים זהו ה' צבאות.

She vowed a vow, and said: "O Lord of Hosts" (I Shemuel 1:11). What is implied by "O Lord of Hosts"? According to R. Judah the son of R. Simon, Chana said to the Holy One, blessed be He: "Master of the universe, there is a host above, and there is a host below. The host above do not eat, nor drink, nor procreate, nor die, but they live forever; and the host below eat, and drink, and procreate, and die. Now I do not know of what host I am, whether I am of the one above or the one below. If I am of the host above, I should not be eating, nor drinking, nor bearing children, nor dying, for I should live forever, just as the host above live forever. But if I am of the host below, then not only should I be eating and drinking, but I should be bearing children and eventually dying, even as the host below eat and drink and procreate and die (Pesikta Rabbati 5:43).

This revelation of a name for God, and with it a new understanding of an aspect of God, is deftly employed by Chana. She knows, as no one before her, that God is Lord of Hosts, Tzva'ot. She describes those hosts. God has created the material and spiritual realm with two hosts who serve Him. The host on high consists of angels, who are immortal. The host below on earth consists of mortals, the Jewish people. Her circumstance is unnatural. Because He is Lord of Hosts, her barrenness is unnatural. She declares to God: *Make up Your mind. Either I am a mortal, as it seems to be because I have a body and I eat and drink. If that is the case, mortals procreate. They create life, for the creation of life is the taste of immortality reserved for mortals. Or I am like the host on high who are immortal and have no need of creating life.*

Chana confronts God with the stark reality that in her barrenness she is a hybrid. Like an immortal angel she does not procreate; like a mortal person she eats and drinks. Her claim is simple: *Either grant me immortality and I will not demand a child; or give me a child because I am mortal.*

In the first, or oldest, version of this *midrash* from Rabbi Eleazar, the claim that Chana makes — based on the notion that the Lord is master of so many hosts — is straightforward. Chana says: *You have so many in your host. Is it so difficult for you to give me a son from one of these?* Rabbi Eleazar lends Chana a parable. Chana is the poor person who has no food, enters a royal banquet, and says to the king, "Given all the food you have here, can't you just give me a bit of something to eat?" When this claim of Chana and its parable reach Rabbi Yehuda, it is given a profoundly new meaning of great theological import. Chana tells God: *You are the master of so many hosts. There is a host, a* tzava, *here below on earth who is mortal. There is a* tzava *in Heaven on high who is immortal.* She is telling God: *You have to choose. If I am a member of the host on high, then there is no problem with my barrenness. The host on high do not procreate and birth. However, the host on high do not eat or drink or die. They are immortal. If the reason You are not giving me a child is because I'm a member of the host on high, then grant me immortality.* On the other hand, Chana plaintively reasons: *If I am a member of the host on earth, well then the host on earth eat, drink, birth, and die. Either grant me immortality, and I will forego my claim to a child, or treat me as a mortal who eats and drinks and knows death. Immortality and barrenness, or mortality and child.*

This passage expresses an idea first found in the Book of Be-Reshit. When Adam and Chava lose immortality for having eaten of the fruit of the Tree of Knowledge, they are immediately given a taste of immortality in the continuity of their lives through children.

The *midrash* closes with Rabbi Yehuda presenting a different version of Rabbi Eleazar's parable.

פסיקתא רבתי (איש שלום) פיסקא-מג כי פקד ה' את חנה דבר אחר ה' צבאות א"ר יהודה ברבי סימון בפעמי רגלים עלתה חנה לב"המק =לבית המקדש= וראתה את כל ישראל שם, אמרה לפני הקדוש ברוך הוא רבונו של עולם כל הצבאות האילו יש לך ואין לי אחד בהם.

Another comment: O Lord of Hosts. R. Judah the son of R. Simon said: On festal pilgrimages, when Chana went up to the Sanctuary, she would see all Israel gathered there. She then said to the Holy One, blessed be He, "Master of the universe, You have all these hosts, but among them not even one is mine" (Pesikta Rabbati 43).

Instead of using the parable of the king and the banquet, Rabbi Yehuda lends greater poignancy. Chana does not make the claim to the king based on a banquet of plentiful food. Rather, she notes that the Temple is filled with Jews. They are the host of God; can God not give her just one of these assembled Jews as a son?

Chana, in these two *midrashim*, tells us what she meant when she named God *Tzeva'ot.* She employs this new name of God to reveal an aspect of His nature as the basis for her claim: *Because you are creator and master of all these hosts, can You not find it in Your heart, You who possess all, You who are master of all these hosts, to give me but one child from the vast richness of Your hosts?*

Rabbi Eleazar further develops her prayerful demand so that we may listen in on her conversation with the Almighty. She turns to God the Creator.

ברכות דף לא עמוד ב

וחנה היא מדברת על לבה אמר רבי אלעזר משום רבי יוסי בן זמרא: על עסקי לבה. אמרה לפניו: רבונו של עולם, כל מה שבראת באשה לא בראת דבר אחד לבטלה, עינים לראות, ואזנים לשמוע, חוטם להריח, פה לדבר, ידים לעשות בהם מלאכה, רגלים להלך בהן, דדים להניק בהן; דדים הללו שנתת על לבי למה, לא להניק בהן? תן לי בן ואניק בהן.

And Chana was speaking in her heart ... Rabbi Eleazar said in the name of Rabbi Yose ben Zimra: [She spoke] about matters of the heart. She said before Him: Master of eternity, of all that You created in a woman you did not create anything in vain — eyes to see, ears to hear, nose to smell, mouth to speak, hands with which to craft, feet to walk with them, breasts to suckle with them. The breasts that you gave me upon my heart, why is it not to nurse with them? Give me a son so that I can nurse with them (Berakhot 31b).

In pain and beauty, this passage speaks for itself. However, the pain and the beauty of this rabbinic passage should not obscure its great idea. The creatorship of God means that life in all its rich detail is purposeful. Creation is not an accident. Each individual life is purposeful. Each and every person has intent. In this speech to God, Chana is portrayed by Rabbi Eleazar as taking her stand on the ground of creation itself. If God does not give her a son to nurse at her breast, then a part of her body — a part of creation — has been created in vain and wasted. The nature of Chana's prayer, of claim and demand, is to hold God to His very own purposes for each element in creation.

There is ample precedent for this. Chana makes demands of the Kadosh Barukh Hu. All such demands must be grounded in God's nature or deeds or promises. Thus the demanding, praying Jew who has a regular and ever-deepening relationship with the one God reminds God of His obligations. The demanding Jew is the faithful and learned Jew.

Yet, this has still deeper roots. God's plan for creation requires a human partner to serve as His custodian of the natural and social realms. Limitation is inherent in partnership. To enter into relationship is to be subject to boundaries. God must ask His partner Moshe for agreement before punishing Israel for sin.

שמות פרשת כי תשא פרק לב (י) וְעַתָּה הַנִּיחָה לִּי וְיִחַר־אַפִּי בָהֶם וַאֲכַלֵּם וְאֶעֱשֶׂה אוֹתְךָ לְגוֹי גָּדוֹל׃

Now, let Me be, that My anger may blaze forth against them ... (Shemot 32:10).

God's plea to Moshe — "let me be" — acknowledges that, because of His partnership with Moshe, He cannot act unilaterally. He needs the agreement of Moshe for any action against the Jewish people. Chana, like Moshe and every person, is God's partner in creation. Her created breasts must nurture a child.

The rabbis have not yet exhausted their portrait of Chana. Her image and stance convince them that she presents not just claim and demand, but moves to direct confrontation.

4

Confrontation

At this point, that all-important description of Chana's prayerful stance before God bears citing again, but this time note in whose company Rabbi Eleazar places Chana. As mentioned above, the simple meaning of the Hebrew *heti'akh* is "hurl." She hurls her words at God. In the Chana context, it describes talking impertinently and insolently to God. Rabbi Eleazar teaches us that Chana is in good company. There are two major figures in TaNaKh — Moshe and Elijah — whose vocation is advocacy to God on behalf of Israel. Rabbi Eleazar teaches that they too hurled their words at God; they too spoke impertinently and insolently. Rabbi Eleazar also cites the case of a post-biblical figure, a rabbinic master, who hurled his words at God on behalf of all Israel suffering through a drought.

תלמוד בבלי מסכת ברכות דף לא עמוד ב
ואמר רבי אלעזר: חנה הטיחה דברים כלפי מעלה, שנאמר: ותתפלל על ה' מלמד, שהטיחה דברים כלפי מעלה. ואמר רבי אלעזר: אליהו הטיח דברים כלפי מעלה, שנאמר: ואתה הסבת את לבם אחרנית. ואמר רבי אלעזר: משה הטיח דברים כלפי מעלה, שנאמר: ויתפלל משה אל ה', אל תקרי אל ה' אלא על ה'...

Rabbi Eleazar said: Chana spoke confrontationally (literally, "hurled words at the One above") to God, as it says, "And Chana prayed upon God." This (*upon* rather than *to*) teaches us that she hurled words at the One above … Rabbi Eleazar also said: Elijah spoke insolently toward Heaven, as it says, "For You did turn their heart backwards …"

Rabbi Eleazar also said: Moshe spoke insolently toward heaven, as it says, "And Moshe prayed upon the Lord." Read not *el* ("to") the Lord, but *al* ("upon") the Lord ... (Berakhot 31b, 32a).

And now to the tale of a rabbi who hurled words at God.

תלמוד בבלי מסכת תענית דף כה עמוד א
לוי גזר תעניתא ולא אתא מיטרא, אמר לפניו: רבונו של עולם! עלית וישבת במרום ואין אתה מרחם על בניך. אתא מיטרא, ואיטלע. אמר רבי אלעזר: לעולם אל יטיח אדם דברים כלפי מעלה, שהרי אדם גדול הטיח דברים כלפי מעלה ואיטלע, ומנו לוי.

Levi ordained a fast, but no rain fell. He thereupon exclaimed: "Master of the universe, You went up and took Your seat on high and You are not merciful to Your children?!" Rain fell but he became lame. R. Eleazar said: Let a man never hurl speech toward God, seeing that one great man did so and he became lame, and he is Levi (Ta'anit 25a).

For his impertinence and insolence, Levi was punished — yet his demand worked and rain came. Rabbi Eleazar characterizes the *tefila* of Chana as confrontational, hurling her words against Heaven itself. This sounds odd and inappropriate for prayer, an activity that is seemingly one directional, from an inferior to a superior. Equals do not bring prayer to each other. They make request. Superiors do not pray to inferiors. *Prayer* is too limited a word for *tefila*, an act that encompasses much more than just a request presented to a superior. *Tefila* begins with prayer but can and often develops into claim, demand, judgment, intercession, confrontation. *Tefila* describes the fullness of communication and interaction in a relationship. Rabbi Eleazar, in portraying Chana's case before God, moves her from reasoning to claim and from demand to confrontation. This stance will now intensify.

Some background to the forthcoming *midrash* is needed. In Bamidbar 5:11-31, the ritual of the *sota* is legislated. If a husband has credible grounds to suspect that his wife has committed adultery because she was seen in seclusion, for a fitting period of time, with another man, the husband can bring his suspicion to the priest in the Beit HaMikdash for resolution. When that happens, the priest implements a trial by ordeal that determines if the suspicion has merit or not. She must drink the waters of the *sota*. The Torah says that if she were adulterous, calamity would overtake her body. However, if the suspicion proves false, she would, as a consequence of the trial by ordeal, conceive and birth a child.

We can now study Chana's boldest confrontation of God.

פסיקתא רבתי (איש שלום) פיסקא-מג כי פקד ה' את חנה

[אם ראה תראה וגו'] (שם /שמואל א' א'/) אם ראה מוטב ואם לאו תראה שלא בטובתך, אמרה לפניו מוטב שתראה בטובה קודם שתראה שלא בטובה, אמרה אם אין אתה פוקדני אני הולכת ועושה עצמי (משחת') [מסתתרת] עם איש אחד, ובעלי רואה אותי וחושדני ומוליכני אצל כהן ומשקה אותי מי המרים, נמצאת אני טהורה ועליך לפקוד אותי וליתן לי בן, שהכתבת בתורה ואם לא נטמאה [וגו'] ונקתה ונזרעה זרע (במדבר ה' כ"ח), הוי אם ראה תראה ראה בטובה עד שלא תראה שלא בטובה.

If in seeing, You will see the affliction of Your servant (I Shemuel 1:11). If You see [my affliction], good; but if not, You will see [my affliction] not to Your good. She said: It is better that You see what pleases You rather than that You see what pleases You not. Hence, she went on to say: If You will not remember me [for a child], I will go and make it appear that I secluded myself with another man; my husband will see me, suspect me of infidelity, take me to a priest, and have me drink the bitter waters of the trial by ordeal given to women suspected of infidelity. I will be found undefiled, and then You will be obliged to remember me and give me a son, because in the Torah You wrote, "If the woman be not defiled … then she shall be cleared, and shall conceive seed" (Numbers 5:28). Hence if in seeing You will see … see when it is good; else You will have to see when it is not (Pesikta Rabbati 43:3, based on Berakhot 31b).

Rare is the case in Hazal of such a determined and brazen attempt to force the hand of God. If God does not give her child, then she will play the suspected adulteress who, when found innocent in the trial by ordeal, becomes pregnant by the waters. God will have no choice but to ensure her pregnancy, lest His words in the Torah be proven false. Chana hurls her words against Heaven. She will coerce God into a miraculous pregnancy by playing the suspected adulteress. Chana uses God's very word, the Torah, to compel God to give her a baby.

5

Opening the Gates

A passage in the Zohar serves as a fitting tribute to the prayerful life of Chana.

זוהר כרך ג (ויקרא) פרשת ויקרא

תא חזי תרין נשין אנון דאשתכחי בעלמא ואמרי תושבחתא דקודשא בריך הוא דכל גוברין דעלמא לא יימרון הכי, ומאן אינון דבורה וחנה, חנה אמרה (שמואל א ב) אין קדוש כיי' כי אין בלתך וכלהו קראי, דהיא פתחא פתחא דמהימנותא לעלמא כגון (שם) מקים מעפר דל מאשפות ירים אביון הא פתחא דמהימנותא להושיבי עם נדיבים הא מהימנותא דלעילא באתר דאבהן שריין, מאן נדיבים אלין אבהן כדכתיב (תהלים מז) נדיבי עמים נאספו.

Come and see: There were two women who existed in the world and uttered praise of the blessed Holy One such as all men of the world could never articulate. Who are they? Devorah and Chana. Chana said, "There is no one holy like Y-H-V-H, for there is no one beside You" (I Shemuel 2:2) — and all those verses [of her song] (I Shemuel 2:1-10). For she opened the gate of faith for the world, for example: He raises the poor from the dust — opening of faith — to seat among nobles (I Shemuel 2:8), faith above, in the place where the patriarchs abide. Who are nobles? The patriarchs, as is said: Nobles of nations have gathered (Psalms 47:10) (Zohar III, 19b).

Building upon Rabbi Eleazar's premise that Chana bequeathed a name — Tzeva'ot — of God that no man had heretofore known or imagined, the Zohar now teaches that there were two women — Devorah and Chana — who reached a level of praise of God never attained by the prayer of a man. Chana opens the gate of faith. As an example, the Zohar quotes a verse from her song, "He raises the poor from the dust / Lifts up the needy from the dunghill / Setting them with nobles / Granting them seats of honor" (I Shemuel 2:8).

Chana raises up the Shekhina for she is a *dal*, an *evion* — impoverished. *Evion* and *dal* represent Shekhina who is always poor of light and in the ashes of the Galut. She is poor of light because she has nothing of her own, but rather receives the flow of emanation from above. Chana, a woman, opens up the gates of faith — which is not just belief as we perceive it, but also the actual experience of God. The Zohar goes on to teach us that through Chana the Shekhina ascends and abides with the patriarchs: He raises the poor from the dust / Lifts up the needy from the dunghill / Setting them with nobles / Granting them seats of honor (I Shemuel 2:8).

In teaching us that, through the prayer of Chana the Shekhina abides with the patriarchs, the Zohar invites us to explore the relationship between Chana and the patriarchs Avraham, Isaac, and Jacob. The Zohar, at the beginning of this passage, does something remarkable. It gives Devorah and Chana a place of common spiritual stature in Israel's sacred history: *There were two women who existed in the world and uttered praise of the blessed Holy One such as all men of the world could never articulate. Who are they? Devorah and Chana.*

In the curatorial act there is reciprocal enlightenment. Chana teaches us something about Devorah. Devorah teaches us something about Chana. Surely the most significant thing they have in common is that they both present a great epic poem and thanksgiving song — the only two women to do so. As the Zohar notes, in their thanksgiving songs they present unprecedented expressions of praise for God. From the placement of Chana we learn that Devorah's song emerges from a life rich in prayer. What does Devorah teach us about Chana? Devorah is the only woman after the patriarchal / matriarchal period — after the narratives of Avraham, Isaac, Jacob, Sarah, Rebecca, Rachel, and Leah — who is given the title Mother in Israel. This is not something we can easily overlook and assign to literary flourish or excited commendation in a great day of victory. The text of Devorah's epic poem tells us that, like Chana, she emerged at a time of difficulty and chaos.

שופטים פרק ה (ו) בִּימֵי שַׁמְגַּר בֶּן עֲנָת בִּימֵי יָעֵל חָדְלוּ אֳרָחוֹת וְהֹלְכֵי
נְתִיבוֹת יֵלְכוּ אֳרָחוֹת עֲקַלְקַלּוֹת: (ז) חָדְלוּ פְרָזוֹן בְּיִשְׂרָאֵל חָדֵלּוּ עַד שַׁקַּמְתִּי
דְּבוֹרָה שַׁקַּמְתִּי אֵם בְּיִשְׂרָאֵל:

In the days of Shamgar son of Anat, in the days of Ya'el, the caravans ceased, those who walked on roads walked on twisting paths. The villagers ceased, they ceased in Israel, until you arose Devorah, you arose a Mother in Israel! (Judges 5:6,7).

After the close of the Torah, after the four matriarchs, no other woman is called a Mother in Israel. Devorah now joins the matriarchs. The Zohar, in associating Chana with Devorah, teaches us that the Jewish people were blessed, if one dare say it, with six matriarchs: Sarah, Rebecca, Rachel, Leah, Devorah, and Chana.

Conclusion

It is time now to step back and appreciate what the rabbis have portrayed in their study of Chana. The rabbis are keenly aware of the testimony that the divine and divinely inspired authors pay to the Jewish reader. The divine author of the Torah and the divinely inspired authors of the Prophets assume an intelligent and probing reader. As with any work of art, the Torah is presented to its audience by the artist. It is entrusted by the artist to the public, in the confidence that the committed and engaged reader will study what is beneath the surface of the painting or the text. Like the other narratives of TaNaKh, the saga of Chana is presented in minimalist language. Imagine if Tolstoy composed the prayerful drama of Chana. It would be pages and pages long!

What have the rabbis done? They read, studied, examined, and probed this brief narrative and its abrupt verbs. They realized that beneath the simple, terse language — "and God closed her womb," or "she cried," or "Chana stood up," or "Chana came forth," or "and she was bitter unto life," etc. — were worlds of meaning and human experience. They know that a person is not hungry, weeping, bitter, hardened of spirit, and driven to enter the Mishkan without a rich, complex personality and great story beneath the surface of the text. To see just the surface in Picasso's *Guernica*, for one example, is to miss the depth of the artist's ideas. This is what Hazal have done with their treatment of this narrative and their portrait of Chana. They have taken us deep beneath the surface of the narrative to expose the inner life of this tormented and praying woman.

Now, perhaps, we can make an observation. The text of TaNaKh is sparse, indeed chary with its details. We know nothing of the first 75 years of Avraham's life. We know nothing of Moshe's childhood in Pharaoh's palace. However, when we meet such figures — because we, like them, are possessed of life experience — we can know certain things without reading them in the text. Chana enters the Mishkan with ease and naturalness, stands in bitterness, speaks to her heart, then emerges into full-fledged intercession with, and indeed demand from, God. These are the practices of a woman who has lived prayer all her life. One cannot enter the Mishkan this way and engage in such confident intercessory prayer without a deep and rich set of lifelong prayer experiences, without a life in proximity to God.

We have described the life and song of Chana in TaNaKh, and Hazal's appreciation of her. With this foundation we can examine the ways in which the rabbis employ Chana to shape our experience of Rosh HaShana and Yom Kippur. Before we proceed, an observation is in order. Hazal assigned no role in *tefila b'tsibur* or *tefilat hatsibur* — communal prayer and prayer on behalf of the community, the Jewish people — to women. How ironic, then, that Hazal establish the practices and inner life setting of *tefila* on the prayerful life of a woman. How ironic that the most awesome experience of *tefila*, the liturgy for the High Holy Days, is shaped by Chana's prayers. While women were not given responsibility for formal mandatory prayer, they were recognized by Hazal as the custodians of *tefila ba'ad hatsibur*, prayer on behalf of the community, the Jewish people. Thus we read of Rachel:

ירמיהו פרק לא (יד) כֹּה אָמַר יְקֹוָק קוֹל בְּרָמָה נִשְׁמָע נְהִי בְּכִי תַמְרוּרִים רָחֵל
מְבַכָּה עַל־בָּנֶיהָ מֵאֲנָה לְהִנָּחֵם עַל־בָּנֶיהָ כִּי אֵינֶנּוּ: (טו) כֹּה אָמַר יְקֹוָק מִנְעִי
קוֹלֵךְ מִבֶּכִי וְעֵינַיִךְ מִדִּמְעָה כִּי יֵשׁ שָׂכָר לִפְעֻלָּתֵךְ נְאֻם־יְקֹוָק וְשָׁבוּ מֵאֶרֶץ אוֹיֵב:
(טז) וְיֵשׁ־תִּקְוָה לְאַחֲרִיתֵךְ נְאֻם־יְקֹוָק וְשָׁבוּ בָנִים לִגְבוּלָם:

> Thus said the Lord: A cry is heard in Ramah — wailing, bitter weeping — Rachel weeping for her children. She refuses to be comforted, for her children, who are gone. Thus said the Lord: Restrain your voice from weeping, your eyes from shedding tears; for there is a reward for your labor — declares the Lord: They shall return from the enemy's land. And there is hope for your future — declares the Lord: Your children shall return to their country (Jeremiah 31:14-16).

The prayers of Rachel are grounded in her motherhood of the Jewish people. She is one of the four matriarchs, mothers of all Israel. Rachel naturally begins her prayerful posture from her national stance. Not so Chana. She comes to this meeting with her God on the ground of her personal barrenness. Chana is that rare religious personality who, out of her personal experience, comes to national advocacy and prayer. In her barrenness she sees the "barrenness" of all Israel. In her life of *tefila* she moves from personal request to national petition. As we have noted, it is the prayers of Chana that move the Jewish people forward at a time when all was chaos and confusion. It is through the *tefilot* of Rosh HaShana and Yom Kippur that the welfare of the Jewish people is secured for the coming year. It is Chana whom the rabbis employ as our guide and inspiration for these *tefilot*. Chana is matriarch of *tefila*, Mother of Prayer.

PART 3
Chana and the Awesome Days

In the liturgical rite, *nusakh* of Eretz Yisrael, the Torah reading for Rosh HaShana makes sense. It is taken from Parashat HaMo'adim, the sacred calendar, in Vayikra 23. It begins with the verses in the Torah that establish Rosh HaShana.

ויקרא פרשת אמור פרק כג (כג) וַיְדַבֵּר יְקֹוָק אֶל מֹשֶׁה לֵּאמֹר: (כד) דַּבֵּר אֶל
בְּנֵי יִשְׂרָאֵל לֵאמֹר בַּחֹדֶשׁ הַשְּׁבִיעִי בְּאֶחָד לַחֹדֶשׁ יִהְיֶה לָכֶם שַׁבָּתוֹן זִכְרוֹן
תְּרוּעָה מִקְרָא קֹדֶשׁ: (כה) כָּל מְלֶאכֶת עֲבֹדָה לֹא תַעֲשׂוּ וְהִקְרַבְתֶּם אִשֶּׁה
לַיקֹוָק:

The Lord spoke to Moshe, saying, "Speak to the Israelite people thus: In the seventh month, on the first day of the month, you shall observe complete rest, a sacred occasion commemorated with loud blasts. You shall not work at your occupations; and you shall bring an offering by fire to the Lord" (Vayikra 23:23-25).

Similar passages in the Torah that present the specific holiday are the readings for Pesakh, Shavuot, Sukkot, and Yom Ha'Kippurim. However, this Torah reading assignment for Rosh HaShana did not long stand. The Talmud in Megilla 31a establishes for all communities and rites the Torah reading for Rosh HaShana.

תלמוד בבלי מסכת מגילה דף לא עמוד א
בראש השנה בחדש השביעי, ומפטירין הבן יקיר לי אפרים, ויש אומרים וה' פקד את שרה, ומפטירין בחנה. והאידנא דאיכא תרי יומי, יומא קמא כיש אומרים ...

> On New Year we read, "On the seventh month," and for Haftara, "Is Ephraim a darling son unto me." According to others, we read, "And the Lord remembered Sarah" and for Haftara the story of Chana. Nowadays that we keep two days, on the first day we follow the ruling of the other authority … (Megilla 31a).

The Talmud selects the narratives of Sarah and Chana as the Torah and Haftara readings for the first day of Rosh HaShana. Hazal select Torah and Haftara readings to ground Rosh HaShana in common human experience. Rosh HaShana commemorates the creation of the world. According to Rabbi Eliezer, Rosh HaShana celebrates the creation of Adam and Chava, the human being.

Creation is unimaginable. Our life experience has no connection to it. It is not an event in Jewish history like the Exodus. It is impossible to see one's being and destiny bound up with Adam and Chava. Unlike the patriarchs and matriarchs, Adam and Chava do not have the regular life experiences that the rest of us know. They are created adults. Therefore, instead of presenting the work of creation and the creation of humanity in the Torah reading for Rosh HaShana, the rabbis present to us (on the first day of Rosh HaShana) the creation of one life — the birth of Isaac to Avraham and Sarah in their old age; and the creation of another life — Shemuel, born to Chana and Elkana. Each woman is barren. Each is given a son by God's will. God continues as the master of creation long after the six days of creation.

In these Torah and Haftara readings the magisterial act of creating, an act reserved exclusively for God, is read into our common human experience: one mother, one father, and one child. We, through the life of the individual person, grasp the universality of humanity.

Why did the rabbis choose the drama of Chana for the Haftara of Rosh HaShana? Why did they juxtapose Chana's experience to Sarah's birth drama as portrayed in the Torah reading? The Talmud presents the following text, which led the rabbis to the determination of the Torah and Haftara readings for the first day of Rosh HaShana.

תלמוד בבלי מסכת ראש השנה דף יא עמוד א

בראש השנה נפקדה שרה רחל וחנה, מנלן? אמר רבי אלעזר: אתיא פקידה פקידה, אתיא זכירה זכירה: כתיב ברחל ויזכר אלהים את רחל, וכתיב בחנה ויזכרה ה', ואתיא זכירה זכירה מראש השנה, דכתיב שבתון זכרון תרועה. פקידה פקידה כתיב בחנה כי פקד ה' את חנה, וכתיב בשרה וה' פקד את שרה.

It was taught in the *baraita*: On Rosh HaShana, Sarah, Rachel, and Chana were revisited by God and conceived children. The Gemara asks: From where do we derive this? Rabbi Eleazar said: This is derived by means of a verbal analogy between one instance of the term "revisiting" (*pekida*) and another instance of the term "revisiting," and by means of a verbal analogy between one instance of the term "remembering" (*zekhira*) and another instance of the word "remembering." It is written about Rachel: "And God remembered Rachel" (Genesis 30:22), and it is written about Chana: "And the Lord remembered her" (I Shemuel 1:19). And the meaning of these instances of the term "remembering" is derived from another instance of the term "remembering," with regard to Rosh HaShana, as it is written: "A solemn rest, a remembrance proclaimed with the blast of a *shofar*" (Leviticus 23:24). From here it is derived that Rachel and Chana were remembered by God on Rosh HaShana. And the meaning of one instance of the term "revisiting" is derived from another instance of the term "revisiting." It is written about Chana: "And the Lord revisited Chana" (I Shemuel 2:21), and it is written about Sarah: "And the Lord revisited Sarah" (Genesis 21:1). From here it is derived that, just as Chana was revisited on Rosh HaShana, so too, Sarah was revisited on Rosh HaShana (Rosh HaShana 11a, Koren Edition).

Rosh HaShana is a day of *zikaron*, a day of memory and remembrance. These three women, Sarah, Rachel, and Chana, after barrenness, were remembered and visited by God and given children on Rosh HaShana. Rosh HaShana is the day of Sarah and Chana. We grasp God's judgment of all humanity on Rosh HaShana, the Yom HaDin, by studying and celebrating God's judgment in visiting Sarah and Chana with child on Rosh HaShana.

With the curatorial act of placing the drama of Chana alongside the narrative of Sarah on Rosh HaShana, the rabbis cross centuries and epics in sacred history to arrange a meeting between these two women: Sarah the first matriarch and Chana the mother of the monarchy are made to meet on Rosh HaShana. What do they say to each other in their annual meeting, the mother of the Jewish people and the mother of Shemuel the nation builder? They meet on holy days commemorating events in the life of the nation their children willed into being. They meet on Rosh HaShana, Judgment Day. The Jewish people stand transfixed as Sarah and Chana walk together, wondering about the meaning of their annual rendezvous. Sarah and Chana, the first and the last of TaNaKh's barren women, are the women of Rosh HaShana.

Through the particular narrative of these two women in the Torah and Haftara readings, we grasp the universality of God's judgment. It is through the particular, the individual experience of one person or several figures in TaNaKh, that the rabbis open a door to Jewish history's drama from exile to redemption.

פסיקתא דרב כהנא (מנדלבוים) פיסקא כ רני עקרה שבע עקרות הן,
שרה רבקה רחל ולאה ואשתו של מנוח וחנה וציון.

There are seven barren ones: Sarah, Rebecca, Rachel, Leah, the wife of Mano'akh, Chana, and Zion (Pesikta de-Rav Kahana 20).

Mark well the seventh barren "woman" is Zion, the Jewish people. Just as the barrenness and redemption of these six women are part of God's plan, so too the "barrenness" of Zion. The first is Sarah. The sixth is Chana. The women of Rosh HaShana are the bookends of the six barren. As these six are "redeemed" with the birth of a child of God's purpose, so too will Zion be redeemed. The barren women carry in their very bodies and births the promise of barren Zion redeemed through the rebirth of her children, the return of the Jewish people. On this day, judgment is pronounced on the nations of the world. God's remembering Sarah and Chana for good judgment on this day is a harbinger of God's redemption of Zion.

It is this decision, to select the drama and prayers of Chana as the Haftara for Rosh HaShana, that had major consequence for the rabbis' understanding of two unique prayers of the Yamim Nora'im, the Days of Awe — Musaf of Rosh HaShana and Ne'ilah. That the rabbis turned to Chana for understanding the meaning and import of these two unique orders of *tefila* should not surprise us.

תלמוד ירושלמי מסכת תענית פרק ב
תשע של ר"ה מניין אמר ר' אבא קרתיגנא כנגד תשע אזכרות שכתוב בפרשת חנה וכתיב בסופה [שמואל א ב י] ה' ידין אפסי ארץ.

The nine [*berakhot*] of Rosh HaShana [Musaf], from where do we gain their meaning? Rabbi Abba of Kartigina said they correspond to the nine invocations of the divine name in the Song of Chana, at the conclusion of which is written: The Lord will judge the ends of the earth (I Shemuel 2:10) (Talmud Yerushalmi Ta'anit 2).

The liturgy is a literary fabric woven of verses of TaNaKh, passages from Hazal, and *tefilot* written by Hazal. The rabbis take these various sources and compose the *nusakh*, or rite, that has come down to us. In the matter of Chana, we are in the process of identifying the distinct passages from TaNaKh, from rabbinic sources, and from the rabbinic pen that have given us the High Holy Day Makhzor, specifically the Musaf, that we have before us. Quite simply, the basic idea of Rosh HaShana is expressed in the Song of Chana as noted by Rabbi Abba: The Lord will judge the ends of the earth (I Shemuel 2:10).

Rosh HaShana is Yom HaDin, the Day of Judgment. Chana celebrates God's judgment that gave her Shemuel. However, it must be understood that Rabbi Abba does not go so far as to say that the source of the unique Musaf of Rosh HaShana — characterized as it is by nine, rather than the traditional seven *berakhot* of Shabbat and the holidays — is actually derived from the Song of Chana, and without that reference we would not know it.

The Musaf for Rosh HaShana was developed by Hazal in the service of the central and only *mitzva* of the day — *shofar* sounding. The *shofar* is sounded in three sets of three voices each. Therefore, Hazal conceived and wrote three unique *berakhot* — Malkhuyot, Zikhronot, and Shofrot — each of which is prelude to each of the three sets of *shofar* sounding. *Prelude* means that a *mitzva* should be performed with intentional and informed devotion. The three unique *berakhot*, or sections, of the Rosh HaShana Musaf teach the meaning and purpose of *shofar* sounding. One of them, Malkhuyot, was incorporated within the traditional middle, or fourth, *berakhah* of the standard Shabbat or holiday Amida, the Kedushat Hayom Berakhah. Thus, the Amida for Rosh HaShana consists of the standard three introductory *berakhot*, the three valedictory *berakhot*, and the three new middle sections: Sovereignty, Remembrances, and Shofar soundings, with the first of these integrated into the fourth, or middle, *berakhah* — hence, the nine *berakhot* that we now enjoy.

The theme of Malkhuyot is the sovereignty of God. The theme of Zikhronot is remembrance. On this day of Rosh HaShana, God remembers the deeds of each person and of each nation, and hands down judgment upon them for the coming year. Zikhronot, as we shall soon see, has special connection to Chana. The theme of Shofrot is that *shofar* sounding inaugurates Jewish sacred history at Sinai and announces redemption in Jerusalem in the Messianic era.

Rabbi Abba suggests that there is a correspondence between Chana's song and these three sections of Musaf. This study of the sources of Rosh HaShana began with the statement that Sarah and Chana were visited, remembered, and judged for good by God — and blessed with a child on Rosh HaShana. From there it followed that the Torah reading for Rosh HaShana is the narrative of Sarah and the Haftara reading is the narrative of Chana. Once that connection is established — once Chana and her drama and song were brought to Rosh HaShana — the rabbis looked at the lives of Sarah and Chana and found important parallels. If these parallels had not been identified, the Haftara would have been different. It is to this that Rabbi Abba of Kartigina draws our attention.

"In the part lies the whole" is a famous statement made by Max Panofsky, the great historian of Gothic architecture. In any given part of a Gothic structure, one can find the whole of Gothic design and art. The same is true for any great system of belief or thought. Its ideas and beliefs are coherent and consistent from setting to setting, from one part to another. The great ideas of Judaism, while having different emphases on different holidays, are nevertheless expressed in each of the holidays, prayers, and, indeed, lifecycle commemorations. What the rabbis look for is coherency and consistency of ideas and beliefs from one Jewish sacred experience to another. The ideas of Rosh HaShana give expression to the beliefs that Chana sings in praise of God.

It is Rabbi Abba of Kartigina who first identifies the verse that is the foundation for this, thus setting us to the task of identifying other parallels between the two. There are nine invocations of the divine name in the Song of Chana. Nine is an *odd* number in both senses of the word. Curiously, it is the months of pregnancy. These nine invocations find correspondence with the nine *berakhot* of Musaf. What characterizes a *berakhah* is the invocation of the divine name.

There are nine *berakhot* in Musaf and nine invocations of the name of God in the Song of Chana.

Yet, for Rabbi Abba of Kartigina, that is not enough. He makes his case for the affinity of the Musaf ideas and the Song of Chana by citing the closing verse of the song, "The Lord will judge the ends of the earth." Chana explicitly declares that God judges humanity. Rosh HaShana is the Day of Judgment for all humanity, to the very ends of the earth. Now that we recognize this idea in the text of Chana's song, we can proceed to identify the other ideas expressed both in the song and in the Musaf service, as first pointed out by Rabbi Abba.

As just noted, the Song of Chana concludes with "God will judge to the very ends of the earth." Rosh HaShana is Yom HaDin, the Day of Judgment, for on this day God judged Adam for his sin and set him free. Thus God desires to do the same for Adam's children, all of humanity. This is the central belief and idea of Rosh HaShana. The Creator, by virtue of His act of creation, is both sovereign and judge.

This idea is expressed in the first unique section of Musaf for Rosh HaShana, Malkhuyot, which is devoted to the sovereignty of God. Malkhuyot culminates in the prayer that, in the End of Days, the sovereignty of God will be recognized by humanity the world over. The acknowledgment of sovereignty is the acceptance of God as judge. In Zikhronot, the second unique section of Musaf for Rosh HaShana, we acknowledge that God is the perfect judge, for He is all knowing. Judgment requires perfect knowledge and memory. It is that perfect memory that God brings to Chana. Remembering her, God will have her conceive and birth a child. Eli affirms that:

שמואל א פרק ב (כא) כִּי־פָקַד יְקֹוָק אֶת־חַנָּה ...

For the Lord remembered Chana … (I Shemuel 2:21).

The judgment of God is heralded in the Heavens above by the sounding of the *shofar*. As it says in the Song of Chana:

שמואל א פרק ב (י) יְקֹוָק יֵחַתּוּ מְרִיבָו עלו עָלָיו בַּשָּׁמַיִם יַרְעֵם...

The foes of the Lord shall be shattered; He will thunder [with *shofar* blasts] against them in the Heavens ... (I Shemuel 2:10).

The Shofrot section describes the first sounding of the *shofar* at Sinai and the future sounding of the *shofar* at the End of Days, when humanity will be judged by God.

Following the *shofar* sounding of each of these three sections of Musaf, the Makhzor proclaims, "*Hayom harat olam*, this day is the world created!" Chana's song in praise of God's omniscience and righteous judgments is grounded in the affirmation of His creatorship. This creatorship is the basis of Rosh HaShana, the Day of Creation. Chana praises God:

שמואל א פרק ב (ח) ...כִּי לַיקֹוָק מְצֻקֵי אֶרֶץ וַיָּשֶׁת עֲלֵיהֶם תֵּבֵל:

For the pillars of the earth are the Lord's; He has set the world upon them (I Shemuel 2:8).

Chana, in the crescendo, grounds her faith in God's creatorship.

God is judge because God is the purposeful Creator. The life of Chana is redolent with the themes of Rosh HaShana — creation, birth, remembrance, and judgment. These are some of the ideas that Chana's song shares with Musaf.

What is most compelling is the unmistakable parallel between the Song of Chana and the Zikhronot section of Musaf. Hazal teach us:

פסיקתא דרב כהנא (מנדלבוים) פיסקא כג ראש השנה

דתניא בתקיעתא דרב זה היום תחילת מעשיך זכרון ליום ראשון וגו'. כי חק לישראל הוא משפט וג' (שם /תהלים/ פא: ה). על המדינות בו יאמר איזו לחרב ואיזו לשלום, איזו לרעב ואיזו לשובע, איזו למות ואיזו לחיים, ובירות בו יפקדו להזכירם חיים ומות ...

In the *shofar* sounding service of the rabbis it is said: This day (of Rosh HaShana) shall ever provide a reminder of the judgment You did pronounce on the first New Year's Day. Therefore on the first day of Tishrei, Rosh HaShana, sentence is pronounced upon the countries of the world, who [is destined] for war and who [is destined] for peace; who [is destined] for famine and who [is destined] for plenty; who [is destined] for death and who [is destined] for life. On this day the lives of mortals are scrutinized to determine who to life and who to death (Pesikta de-Rav Kahana 23).

This *midrash* is the source of Zikhronot, the middle section of the Musaf.

אַתָּה זוֹכֵר מַעֲשֵׂה עוֹלָם וּפוֹקֵד כָּל יְצוּרֵי קֶדֶם
לְפָנֶיךָ נִגְלוּ כָּל תַּעֲלוּמוֹת וַהֲמוֹן נִסְתָּרוֹת שֶׁמִּבְּרֵאשִׁית.
כִּי אֵין שִׁכְחָה לִפְנֵי כִסֵּא כְבוֹדֶךָ וְאֵין נִסְתָּר מִנֶּגֶד עֵינֶיךָ:
אַתָּה זוֹכֵר אֶת כָּל הַמִּפְעָל. וְגַם כָּל הַיְצוּר לֹא נִכְחַד מִמֶּךָּ:
הַכֹּל גָּלוּי וְיָדוּעַ לְפָנֶיךָ ה' אלקינו, צוֹפֶה וּמַבִּיט עַד סוֹף כָּל הַדּוֹרוֹת.
כִּי תָבִיא חוֹק זִכָּרוֹן לְהִפָּקֵד כָּל רוּחַ וָנֶפֶשׁ .
לְהִזָּכֵר מַעֲשִׂים רַבִּים וַהֲמוֹן בְּרִיּוֹת לְאֵין תַּכְלִית:
מֵרֵאשִׁית כָּזֹאת הוֹדָעְתָּ, וּמִלְּפָנִים אוֹתָהּ גִּלִּיתָ .
זֶה הַיּוֹם תְּחִלַּת מַעֲשֶׂיךָ, זִכָּרוֹן לְיוֹם רִאשׁוֹן .
כִּי חוֹק לְיִשְׂרָאֵל הוּא מִשְׁפָּט לאלקי יַעֲקֹב:
וְעַל הַמְּדִינוֹת בּוֹ יֵאָמֵר אֵיזוֹ לַחֶרֶב, וְאֵיזוֹ לַשָּׁלוֹם,
אֵיזוֹ לָרָעָב, וְאֵיזוֹ לָשֹׂבַע ,
וּבְרִיּוֹת בּוֹ יִפָּקֵדוּ לְהַזְכִּירָם לְחַיִּים וְלַמָּוֶת.
מִי לֹא נִפְקַד כְּהַיּוֹם הַזֶּה. כִּי זֵכֶר כָּל הַיְצוּר לְפָנֶיךָ בָּא.
מַעֲשֵׂה אִישׁ וּפְקֻדָּתוֹ וַעֲלִילוֹת מִצְעֲדֵי גָבֶר .

מַחְשְׁבוֹת אָדָם וְתַחְבּוּלוֹתָיו וְיִצְרֵי מַעַלְלֵי אִישׁ:

You remember the creation works of the world / and judge all artistically fashioned of yore.

Before You is revealed everything hidden / and a multitude of mysteries from the creation beginning.

For there is no forgetfulness before Your weighty throne / and there is nothing hidden from Your eyes.

You remember everything created / and indeed all that is artistically fashioned is not hidden from You.

Everything is revealed and known before You God / You peer and gaze to the end of all generations.

When You bring forth the ways of remembrance / to judge all spirit and life.

To bring to memory a wealth of deeds / and a multitude of creatures limitless.

From creation time You made this known / and from the very beginning You revealed this.

This day marks the beginning of Your creation / it is a remembrance of the first day.

For this is the way of Israel / a law of the God of Jacob.

And upon the nations of the world, on this day it is pronounced / who to the sword and who to peace?

Who to famine and who to satisfaction?

And creatures are judged on this day / to remember them for life and for death.

Who is it that is not judged on this very day / for the remembrance of all artistically fashioned comes before You.

The works of every person and their record / and the accomplishments of everyone's path.

The thoughts of every person and their plans / and the artistry of the designs of every person.

These antonymic juxtapositions or inversions — war and peace, famine and plenty, life and death — constitute the literary structure of Chana's epic song. She presents to us the starkly opposing judgments and fates that face every human and every nation: life or death, the world below or the world above, wealth or poverty, plenty or famine. Hazal, who conceived, developed, and wrote the Zikhronot section of the Musaf service for Rosh HaShana, drew upon this literary device found in the Song of Chana. Appropriately, Chana closes her song in praise of God's judgment, "The Lord will judge to the ends of the earth."

Where else do we find words and ideas like these on Rosh HaShana and Yom Kippur? In what other *tefilot* are we summoned to consider that God is judge, and, as we stand before God, we acknowledge that the coming year fills us with awe and dread? Will it be a year of life or death, of poverty or riches, of peace or war, of the sword or the book, of health or illness? The poem Unetane Tokef, which translates to "Let us present the power of the sanctity of this day," expresses these ideas as no other prayer does. Its words speak for themselves.

וּנְתַנֶּה תֹּקֶף קְדֻשַּׁת הַיּוֹם כִּי הוּא נוֹרָא וְאָיֹם
וּבוֹ תִּנָּשֵׂא מַלְכוּתֶךָ וְיִכּוֹן בְּחֶסֶד כִּסְאֶךָ
אֱמֶת כִּי אַתָּה הוּא דַיָּן ...
וְכוֹתֵב וְחוֹתֵם וְסוֹפֵר וּמוֹנֶה
וְתִזְכֹּר כָּל הַנִּשְׁכָּחוֹת וְתִפְתַּח אֶת סֵפֶר הַזִּכְרוֹנוֹת
וּמֵאֵלָיו יִקָּרֵא וְחוֹתָם יַד כָּל אָדָם בּוֹ ...
וְיֹאמְרוּ הִנֵּה יוֹם הַדִּין ...
וְכָל בָּאֵי עוֹלָם יַעַבְרוּן לְפָנֶיךָ כִּבְנֵי מָרוֹן ...
וְתַחְתֹּךְ קִצְבָה לְכָל בְּרִיָּה וְתִכְתֹּב אֶת גְּזַר דִּינָם
בְּרֹאשׁ הַשָּׁנָה יִכָּתֵבוּן וּבְיוֹם צוֹם כִּפּוּר יֵחָתֵמוּן
כַּמָּה יַעַבְרוּן וְכַמָּה יִבָּרֵאוּן
מִי יִחְיֶה וּמִי יָמוּת
מִי בְקִצּוֹ וּמִי לֹא בְּקִצּוֹ
מִי בַמַּיִם וּמִי בָאֵשׁ
מִי בַחֶרֶב וּמִי בַחַיָּה
מִי בָרָעָב וּמִי בַצָּמָא

מִי בָרַעַשׁ וּמִי בַמַּגֵּפָה
מִי בַחֲנִיקָה וּמִי בַסְּקִילָה
מִי יָנוּחַ וּמִי יָנוּעַ
מִי יִשָּׁקֵט וּמִי יְטֹּרֵף
מִי יִשָּׁלֵו וּמִי יִתְיַסָּר
מִי יֵעָנִי וּמִי יֵעָשִׁיר
מִי יֻשְׁפַּל וּמִי יָרוּם

We shall ascribe intense holiness to this day.
For it is awesome and frightening.
In truth You are the judge…
He who inscribes and seals,
Remembering all that is forgotten.
You open the book of remembrance
Which proclaims itself,
And the seal of each person is there.
Behold the Day of Judgment …
And all creatures shall parade before You …
As a shepherd herds his flock,
Decreeing the length of their days,
Inscribing their judgment.
On Rosh HaShana it is inscribed,
And on Yom Kippur it is sealed.
How many shall pass away and how many shall be born,
Who shall live and who shall die,
Who shall reach the end of his days and who shall not,
Who shall perish by water and who by fire,
Who by sword and who by wild beast,
Who by famine and who by thirst,
Who by earthquake and who by plague,
Who by strangulation and who by stoning,
Who shall have rest and who shall wander,
Who shall be at peace and who shall be pursued,
Who shall be at rest and who shall be tormented,
Who shall become rich and who shall be impoverished,
Who shall be exalted and who shall be brought low.

The last two antonymic destinies are taken from the Song of Chana.

שמואל א פרק ב (ז) יְקֹוָק מוֹרִישׁ וּמַעֲשִׁיר מַשְׁפִּיל אַף־מְרוֹמֵם:

The Lord makes poor and makes rich; He casts down, He also lifts high (I Shemuel 2:7).

Not to speak of the awesome dread of the opening lines, "Who shall live, and who shall die," which echo Chana's poetry:

שמואל א פרק ב (ו) יְקֹוָק מֵמִית וּמְחַיֶּה מוֹרִיד שְׁאוֹל וַיָּעַל:

The Lord deals death and gives life … (I Shemuel 2:6).

This awesome prayer is followed by the Kedusha, in which we recite, "Kadosh, Kadosh, Kadosh, Holy, Holy, Holy," three times. Chana's song of stark choice judgments, nine of them to be sure, begins with the declaration that God is Kadosh. Her song closes with the affirmation that on Judgment Day the *shofar* is sounded. Following our recitation of Kedusha, we continue with the Musaf Amida, and like Chana we acknowledge with the *shofar*. This unique Musaf is also *tefilat* Chana.

Ne'ilah: As the Gates Close

The Unetane Tokef prayer is a bridge from Rosh HaShana to Yom Kippur. These two holy days share this awesome *tefila,* whose ideas originate in the Song of Chana. Before Chana proposes the contract with God that gains her a child, we are told nothing about the content of her *tefilot* but a good deal about what the High Priest Eli saw as she prayed. He noticed that Chana increased her prayer. He was acutely aware of the length of her prayer, and especially of its silence. Had she prayed aloud, had her lips birthed words and chant, had her body swayed to the rhythm of her voice, he would not have been so confounded. He would have known what she was doing in his Mishkan. She prayed for a long time. As the length of her prayer increased, she immersed herself ever more deeply in the presence, in the silence.

The liturgy of Yom Kippur is distinguished in many ways. One of them is the unique Ne'ilah service. On every holiday we offer Ma'ariv, Shaharit, Musaf, and Mincha. As the gates of the Temple and the Gates of Heaven are about to close, as the sun is about to set, we offer an additional prayer, unique to Yom Kippur: Ne'ilah, meaning "the closing of the gates." The rabbis in the Talmud Yerushalmi want to know the basis of this prayer.

תלמוד ירושלמי מסכת תענית פרק ד
מניין לנעילה ... ר' חייא בשם ר' יוחנן ר' שמעון בן חלפתא בשם ר"מ [שמואל א א יב] והיה כי הרבתה להתפלל לפני ה' מכאן שכל המרבה בתפלה נענה:

What is the source of the Ne'ilah service? Rabbi Meir said: "It is written, 'And it was as she increased her prayer in the presence of God ...' This tells us that whoever increases in prayer will be heard and accepted" (I Shemuel 1:12) (Talmud Yerushalmi Ta'anit 4).

Rabbi Meir teaches that, on the holiest day of the year, Yom Kippur, when we are most in need of God's receiving our prayer, we should turn to Chana for inspiration and instruction. We should increase our prayer. We add an additional service. This means that, not only does Chana teach us the ways of prayer, not only is her song the source of some of the critical ideas of Rosh HaShana, but she has something else to offer us. She portrays the transformation of a normal person into a *mitpalelet*, a praying person. As we pray at Ne'ilah, we are expected to become like Chana. Ne'ilah is *tefilat* Chana.

Ne'ilah is offered by a unique community. It is a Jewish community that emerges once a year, for just an hour or so as the sun is setting, at a time that is neither day nor night, as the Gates are about to close. Yom Kippur is a day suffused with light. It is a day of purity. When a Jew finally arrives at the Ne'ilah service, he or she is cleansed of all sin, forgiven and pure. This presents an opportunity to pray in the most noble manner possible.

By the time a Jew arrives at Ne'ilah, there is really nothing left for which to pray. The Vidui, the Yom Kippur acknowledgment of sin, has been recited eight times. Israel is cleansed of her sins. We have emptied our hearts and minds and souls of all our needs. What is left? Ne'ilah is *tefila* for the sake of *tefila*. It is prayer for the sake of prayer. It seeks nothing but its own expression. It is the purest of all *tefilot*. It is *tefila* in standing before the Kadosh Barukh Hu. The community, the Jewish people who pray Ne'ilah, are the community of *tzadikim*, the community of the perfectly righteous. After all, for the previous twenty-four hours the Jewish people the world over have fasted; have separated themselves from the world; have set aside their daily life struggle; have immersed themselves in the prayer book and Torah reading; and have reconciled with God and their fellow Jews, family, friends, neighbors, and community.

Chana increased her prayer before God. As Yom Kippur and its light slip away, we stand in this moment of prayer increase as Chana did long ago at Shilo. Service by service, prayer by prayer, hour after hour we have increased our prayer on this the day of Israel's great fast. At Ne'ilah time, we are in the depths of prayer, and out of those depths we call upon the Name.

When Chana returns to Shilo to fulfill her oath to bring Shemuel to the service of God, Eli the High Priest does not recognize her. She is now a mother, filled with joy and purpose. The last time he saw Chana, she was immersed in tears and bitterness, a woman of hardened spirit. Now transformed, Eli no longer recognizes her. Chana has to remind him that he has seen her before. He has in the past taken powerful note of her. She presents two forms of identification. She first reminds him that she is the *mitpalelet*, the one who judges and intercedes through prayer with God. He must surely remember. It was so uncommon that, at the time, he did not know what she was doing. She also tells us something new: When she engaged in *tefila* she was the woman *hanitzevet*, the woman of standing. She was the *nitzevet* in the Mishkan before the Kadosh Barukh Hu.

At the foot of Mount Sinai, when Israel receives the Torah and enters into the *brit*, they are *nitzavim*. Chana is the *mitpalelet*. She is the *nitzevet*. As the *nitzevet*, she transforms the nature of the place in which she stands. She takes *place* from the prosaic and moves it to the sacred.

The first time in the Torah we encounter the other word for "standing" — *amida*, as in the Amida prayer — is when Avraham stands before and in the presence of the Kadosh Barukh Hu, as it is written:

בראשית פרשת וירא פרק יח וְהוּא־עֹמֵד עֲלֵיהֶם תַּחַת הָעֵץ וַיֹּאכֵלוּ

and he (Avraham) stood before them (the divine presence) under the tree … (Be-Reshit 18:8).

In the presence, Avraham stands again and again.

בראשית פרשת וירא פרק יח וְאַבְרָהָם עוֹדֶנּוּ עֹמֵד לִפְנֵי יְקֹוָק:

… while Avraham remained standing before the Lord (Be-Reshit 18:22).

בראשית פרשת וירא פרק יט (כז) וַיַּשְׁכֵּם אַבְרָהָם בַּבֹּקֶר אֶל־הַמָּקוֹם אֲשֶׁר־עָמַד שָׁם אֶת־פְּנֵי יְקֹוָק:

Next morning, Avraham hurried to the place where he had stood before the Lord ... (Be-Reshit 19:27).

In this first great prayer of intercession, Avraham is in *amida*. He takes his stance in the presence. Mark well, three times the Torah presents his *amida*, his standing.

Later in the Torah, when Moshe describes his experience at Sinai, he tells us:

דברים פרשת ואתחנן פרק ה (ה) אָנֹכִי עֹמֵד בֵּין־יְקֹוָק וּבֵינֵיכֶם בָּעֵת הַהִוא לְהַגִּיד לָכֶם אֶת־דְּבַר יְקֹוָק

I stood between the Lord and you at that time to convey the Lord's words to you ... (Devarim 5:5).

Furthermore, Moshe tells the Jewish people:

דברים פרשת ואתחנן פרק ה (כח) וְאַתָּה פֹּה עֲמֹד עִמָּדִי וַאֲדַבְּרָה אֵלֶיךָ אֵת כָּל־הַמִּצְוָה וְהַחֻקִּים וְהַמִּשְׁפָּטִים אֲשֶׁר תְּלַמְּדֵם ...

But you, Moshe, stand here with Me, and I will give you the whole — the laws and the rules that you shall teach them ... (Devarim 5:28).

This brings us to an important feature of this distinguished service. Ne'ilah is offered in both its silent and public recitation while standing in the presence. Ne'ilah happens when a Jew takes steps to enter into and transform a place. The praying person transforms place into the *makom* of standing in the presence.

שמואל א פרק א (כו) וַתֹּאמֶר בִּי אֲדֹנִי חֵי נַפְשְׁךָ אֲדֹנִי אֲנִי הָאִשָּׁה הַנִּצֶּבֶת עִמְּכָה בָּזֶה לְהִתְפַּלֵּל אֶל־יְקֹוָק:

And so she says to him, "Please my lord, as you live my lord, I am the woman who stood here beside you and prayed to the Lord (I Shemuel 1:26).

Chana identifies herself as the one who stood before God at the Mishkan in *tefila*. The Ne'ilah service concludes with the same image.

אתה הבדלת אנוש מראש ותכירהו לעמוד לפניך

From the very beginning of creation you have distinguished only the human to stand before you (Yom Kippur Ne'ilah service).

No other Jewish prayer carries the introduction and the invocation: We who now enter into prayer stand before God and stand in the presence. Only the one created in the *tselem elokim,* the image of God, is recognized by God to stand before Him. The opening words of the unique portion of the Ne'ilah service declare our standing before the One. At Ne'ilah we stand before God as Chana did long ago at Shilo.

Rabbi Meir tells us that we derive the meaning of Ne'ilah from the experience of Chana. Ne'ilah is the prayer of Chana, *tefilat* Chana. We are summoned like her to become known as the person who stands before God. Ne'ilah is the prayer of the *tzadik*, the perfectly righteous.

ישעיהו פרק ס (כ) לֹא־יָבוֹא עוֹד שִׁמְשֵׁךְ וִירֵחֵךְ לֹא יֵאָסֵף כִּי יְקֹוָק יִהְיֶה־לָּךְ לְאוֹר עוֹלָם וְשָׁלְמוּ יְמֵי אֶבְלֵךְ: (כא) וְעַמֵּךְ כֻּלָּם צַדִּיקִים לְעוֹלָם יִירְשׁוּ אָרֶץ נֵצֶר מטעו מַטָּעַי מַעֲשֵׂה יָדַי לְהִתְפָּאֵר:

Your sun shall set no more, your moon no more expire; for the Lord shall be a light to you forever, and your days of mourning shall be ended. And your people, all of them righteous, shall possess the land for all time; they are the shoot that I planted, My handiwork in which I glory (Isaiah 60:20-21).

Afterword

Chana Tova Poupko נ״ע was brought home to Eretz Yisrael, to her great-grandparents, Rabbi Baruch and Hinda Poupko ז״ל and Rabbi Herman and Helen Davis ז״ל, fulfilling the imperative of Jacob:

וְעָשִׂיתָ עִמָּדִי חֶסֶד וֶאֱמֶת אַל נָא תִקְבְּרֵנִי בְּמִצְרָיִם ...
וְשָׁכַבְתִּי עִם אֲבֹתַי וּנְשָׂאתַנִי מִמִּצְרַיִם וּקְבַרְתַּנִי בִּקְבֻרָתָם...

She abides there with them until that day known only to the Kadosh Barukh Hu when she will again present her personal *tefila,* which became our national *shir*.

וַתִּתְפַּלֵּל חַנָּה וַתֹּאמַר עָלַץ לִבִּי בַּיקֹוָק רָמָה קַרְנִי בַּיקֹוָק ...
יְקֹוָק מֵמִית וּמְחַיֶּה מוֹרִיד שְׁאוֹל וַיָּעַל ...
רַגְלֵי חֲסִידָיו יִשְׁמֹר ...
יְקֹוָק יָדִין אַפְסֵי אָרֶץ וְיִתֶּן עֹז לְמַלְכּוֹ וְיָרֵם קֶרֶן מְשִׁיחוֹ...